Career Rehab is the guide I needed in the help you challenge your fears and step up to your career dreams. You owe it to yourself to pursue a career that meets your needs.

—MINDA HARTS, CEO OF THE MEMO, LLC AND AUTHOR OF *THE MEMO: WHAT WOMEN OF COLOR NEED TO KNOW TO SECURE A SEAT AT THE TABLE*

Choosing a career is not a one-time event, but continuous as you learn what you enjoy and unlearn what's holding you back from getting there. Much of what helps us succeed in our career can end up limiting our ability to adapt in the future. Kanika understands this and has developed the mindset, methods, and models to help you break free of what's holding you back to achieve whatever you aim for.

—BARRY O'REILLY, FOUNDER OF EXECCAMP, BUSINESS ADVISOR, AND AUTHOR OF *UNLEARN* AND *LEAN ENTERPRISE*

We all dream about the perfect job or the perfect career, but there can be all sorts of obstacles that get in the way of our finding it. And when we do find it, we may be surprised that we're afraid to take the leap. In her powerful book *Career Rehab*, Kanika Tolver provides you with all the tools you need to not just find the career of your dreams, but to confidently embrace it. With Kanika as your guide and mentor, you can do it!

—PETER ECONOMY, THE LEADERSHIP GUY

When you are ready to take your career to the next level, *Career Rehab* is the resource guide for you. It is a guidebook full of great resources to shift your career to the next level. Elevate yourself and your career by investing in *Career Rehab*!

—ARQUELLA HARGROVE, CEO, EPIC COLLABORATIVE ADVISORS

Kanika Tolver has written an extraordinary guide to professional development. Read her book and learn the best ways to create the dream career you have always desired.

—COURTENEY VICTORIA CRAWLEY-DYSON, CEO AND GRAPHIC DESIGNER, THE KAIROS GRAPHICS DESIGNS

Many of us have caught ourselves drifting off mentally and fantasizing about "what might have been" in our careers and in our lives. Kanika is one of those unique people who can inspire you to stop daydreaming and start planning how to reinvent yourself. Her book offers practical ways to channel your life experience and career history into something new and better. Think of this book as a way to get virtual coaching from a professional who specializes in helping people improve their earning potential AND their quality of life. Pick up these pages packed with encouragement and insight if you want to stop dreaming and start realizing your next career shift.

—BOBBY ALLEN, CHIEF TECHNOLOGY OFFICER, CLOUDGENERA

In a hectic, competitive career environment, sustainable success requires targeted strategy and actionable advice. *Career Rehab* provides the tools to create a thriving work life that fuels a rewarding personal life.

—DALAN VANTERPOOL, CEO AND EXECUTIVE CAREER COACH, DV GLOBAL GROUP

This book helped me realize my potential to go after my dreams relentlessly while transitioning from a banker to an engineer in the tech industry. *Career Rehab* also helped me create a personal brand that has opened up new doors for me.

—BROADUS PALMER, FOUNDER, LEVEL UP WITH BROADUS

CAREER REHAB

rebuild your
personal brand
and **rethink**
the way you work

kanika tolver

Entrepreneur Press®

Entrepreneur Press, Publisher
Cover Design: Andrew Welyczko
Production and Composition: Eliot House Productions

This publication is designed to provide accurate and authoritative information
in regard to the subject matter covered. It is sold with the understanding
that the publisher is not engaged in rendering legal, accounting, or other
professional services. If legal advice or other expert assistance is required, the
services of a competent professional person should be sought.

Entrepreneur Press® is a registered trademark of Entrepreneur Media, Inc.

Library of Congress Cataloging-in-Publication Data
  Names: Tolver, Kanika, author.
  Title: Career rehab : rebuild your personal brand and rethink the way you
     work / by Kanika Tolver.
  Description: Irvine, California : Entrepreneur Media, Inc., [2020] |
     Summary: "Professional career coach and motivational speaker Kanika
     Tolver helps reader rethink, re-vision, and rehab their careers using a
     strategic action plan focused on building a personal brand that
     maximizes and monetizes their core skills"-- Provided by publisher.
  Identifiers: LCCN 2019032480 | ISBN 978-1-59918-651-1 (paperback) |
     ISBN 978-1-61308-412-0 (ebook)
  Subjects: LCSH: Career development. | Career changes.
  Classification: LCC HF5381 .T6127 2020 | DDC 650.1--dc23
  LC record available at https://lccn.loc.gov/2019032480

Dedication

GOD without you I am nothing. Thank you for loving me.

To my husband Byron Tolver and parents Kelly and Alton Harris; I thank God for your support and love. Special thank you to my late grandmother Juanita Brown for teaching me how to lead and serve others.

To all of the book contributors and my career coaching clients, whom I thank for working with me on this book project. I hope we can continue to teach the world how to rehab careers.

☆ ☆ ☆

CONTENTS

CHAPTER 2

CAREER REHAB: THE DIAGNOSIS. 13

CHAPTER 3

REPOSITION YOURSELF. 23

CHAPTER 4

THE REHAB YOU CAREER BLUEPRINT 41

☆ ☆ ☆

FOREWORD

by Dr. Patti Fletcher
founder of PSDNetwork, LLC, speaker, and author of
Disrupters: Success Strategies from Women Who Break the Mold

What does the word "rehab" mean to you? It's one of those words that can take on different personalities depending on the situation. It can mean that you are changing a system of habits (often ones you need to break for your health or personal wellbeing). It can also refer to a renovation: one that is physical (as with a home rehab) or personal (if you are making moves to change your life). No matter how you use it, though, the word "rehab" is all about change. And change is challenging.

Change is my business. As an entrepreneur, category creator, speaker, author, and coach, I spend a lot of time talking with leaders and their teams about how to disrupt the habits, behaviors, and systems standing in their way of creating communities of change leaders with common visions. And yes—sometimes the changes these teams need to make to rehab their businesses and companies are not easy ones to make. But is anything that's truly worth it ever easy to come by? Most times, you need to put in the work to get the reward. That's what the word "rehab" is all about—stripping something down to the basic framework and doing the hard work of rebuilding your dream vision, whether that's a house, a business, or even a career.

That's what Kanika Tolver does for her clients. She takes her clients' careers in her hands and strips away what is holding them back from achieving success, looking for the "good bones" that they can use to create a new vision for their working lives. Together, they reframe what it means to be a professional by building a new career brand based on the best features of their resume.

In *Career Rehab*, Kanika brings her career coaching expertise directly to her readers. After working in the tech industry (both in the private sector and for the government), Kanika found that the best way to expand and enhance her own career brand was to boldly interact with companies as a *personal* brand. To that end, she encourages her clients to create a brand identity, to "date" jobs until they find one that fits, to boldly claim their worth both ideologically and financially, and to never settle until they get their professional house in order.

That's something that really speaks to me. As a known disrupter (I wrote a book called *Disrupters*, after all), I am on board with the idea of shaking up the status quo at work. Why not? The only people for whom the status quo really works are the gatekeepers who enforce the rules. And people have their bottom line at the top of their priority list—not necessarily their employees. In today's competitive job market, the status quo just doesn't work anymore—especially for women and other under-represented populations. Kanika knows that, which is why she has spent years focusing on helping rising professionals, career dropouts, and budding entrepreneurs engage with what makes them unique to rebuild their careers and lives.

So, are you ready to rehab your career? If you are, then think of this book as your blueprint. With Kanika's guidance, you are going to take a sledgehammer to knock down the walls that are boxing you in. You are going to tear away what no longer works for you—the long commute, the lower-than-you'd like wage, the toxic team—and get down to the foundation of what you *do* want. You are going to create new spaces for yourself and let in a little light. You are going to dust off that old resume and make it shine like a new floor. You are going to build a new career brand that gets you the job you've always dreamed of. You are going to build your "next big thing" right now.

☆ ☆ ☆

INTRODUCTION

When you think of the word *rehab*, what comes to mind? Do you think of words like *addiction*, or perhaps *restoration* or *rebuilding*? Whether you think of rehab in terms of personal issues or the rehabbing and restoration of a home, the word is often tied to improving something that is not healthy in its current state. Now add the word *career*. Is it an odd combination? Of course it is. The word *career* feels positive and forward-looking, while *rehab* may evoke negative emotions. While the phrase seems somewhat dissonant, there are many professionals across the world who are having negative career experiences and failing to advance. They need career rehab to renovate and re-envision their careers into ones that will carry them into the next phase of their lives.

Career Rehab is all about eliminating confusion and finding happiness. Whether you are a college graduate, current professional, or retiree, you can create a career you will love. *Career Rehab* will equip you to brand yourself like a product, "date" jobs to build your personal brand, network like a hustler, and get the pay you deserve. You are going to take the "good bones" of your career, strip away what no longer works, and turn it into a career that gives you success and joy for the long term.

The great thing about the concept of career rehab is that it works for the average professional, who may have given up and now believes they will never have the career they want. Deep down, they are looking for a solution. Maybe you are ready to get the promotion you want or you are ready for a career change. Then career rehab is for YOU. Or maybe you are a college student and want to make sure your passion aligns with your first job out of college or with the first few years in your industry. Career rehab is for YOU, too.

Think about it like this. The process of building a solid career is very similar to building a new house; professionals need the right foundation to maintain a career that they can brand, market, and sell. The homes that usually sell fast make families feel happy. They have the right size rooms, a nice yard, and a beautiful kitchen. Employees too are looking for companies that will create a happy career experience for them—ones that offer the right incentives, work-life balance, and fair compensation. In this book, you will learn that it's not the companies' responsibility to make you happy; it's *your* job to find and create career happiness for yourself. Too often professionals put their trust and career goals in the hands of bad managers, only to be disappointed. But career rehab can help you recover and give you the confidence to land your dream job.

Are You Satisfied?

The Conference Board's 2018 survey on job satisfaction found that 51 percent of U.S. employees are satisfied with their current jobs. That's not a great ratio—it seems that a lot of people are decidedly unhappy at work. Some of the biggest disappointments mentioned were limited professional development and lack of recognition for a job well done. So slightly less than half the U.S. work force wants more training classes, better performance policies, and performance bonuses. The lack of training and performance bonuses makes some professionals feel worthless, which leads to bad morale. Bad morale in turn leads to a bad attitude and poor communication with your teammates and leadership team, which affects not only how you do your job, but how those around you do theirs. This is why many professionals need career rehab.

As a professional career coach, I love helping people restore their careers. I have coached more than 500 professionals and interviewed HR experts, industry leaders, and other career coaches trying to figure out why people are so unhappy with their jobs. And yes, I have been in career rehab myself. Throughout my own journey toward career happiness, I read hundreds of career-development articles and books, hoping to find the magic formula for career happiness. Many of them instructed people on how to get a job, but the real challenge was figuring out how to find a job that is the right fit. I ultimately found that there is no magic bullet. You have to do the hard work of rehabbing your career to make it match your vision.

My career-coaching practice, Career Rehab LLC, is in Washington, DC, and I have worked with clients in the private sector, federal government, and nonprofit organizations. Most of my clients want to create a career blueprint for themselves so they can meet their goals in a way that works with their lives. For example, as I have worked to help my clients get a better job or change careers, a reasonable commute has been a high-ranking request in the past three years—and there is good reason for that. *Business Insider* reported in 2017 that adding 20 minutes to a daily commute not only makes people miserable, but also amounts to the same feeling you get after receiving a pay cut of around 19 percent. People are tired of job offers without a pay raise or with a 90-minute commute. This is just one of many issues I address with my clients—helping professionals identify the roles that offer reasonable commutes and more compensation (which I refer to as "commutes worth the coins").

Employees Who Need Career Rehab

I have identified three types of people who need to get their professional houses in order with career rehab. First up are the *cool geeks*. These people have recently graduated from college or have less than five years of work experience. I help the cool geeks stop feeling worthless, define their career blueprint, network like a hustler, and learn how to "date" jobs (which I'll talk more about in Chapter 6).

Then we have the next group: the *corporate rebels*, who have been working in a job they don't like and are ready to go against the grain and make a change in their career. Usually I assist corporate rebels with breaking up with their jobs and landing new jobs with a better company culture and a higher salary.

Last we have the *career dropouts*. These are the professionals who have worked 10 years or more in an industry and are ready for a career change—or they are ready to retire and start a business or new career.

In this book, I will show you how to be authentic and sell your personal brand as a cool geek, corporate rebel, or career dropout.

What to Expect in This Book

To help showcase how rehabbing your career can work no matter where you are in life, I'll be sharing some success stories from my star clients and experts in the career-development field. I can't wait to share how I coached Courteney Crawley-Dyson (cool geek), a graphics-design student in community college. I taught her how to build her online portfolio and land her first job working as a graphics designer for a high-profile federal government organization, where her design work was featured on Capitol Hill. You'll also meet my client Darrell Dreher Jr. (corporate rebel), an information technology professional who was unhappy at a smaller IT company and was ready to land his dream job at Microsoft. I rebranded his resume and coached him throughout the salary negotiation process so he could land a six-figure job as a senior technical account manager. I will share with you how he learned to network like a hustler and get the pay he deserved as a minority male. Then there's Malcolm Thomas (IT cool geek), a military veteran and security guard who wanted to get into the tech industry. He enrolled in my coaching program, and within two months he was a certified database administrator making six figures at a nonprofit organization. Malcolm was ready to rehab his career so he could give his wife and two children a better life. Later in this book, I will walk you through how each one of these professionals graduated from my career rehab programs with my guidance and expertise.

Throughout the book, I will also highlight authors, career coaches, and industry influencers whom I consider career rehab experts. These profound individuals have successfully career-coached others, developed much-needed diversity and inclusion programs, and written career-development books. Career-rehab experts have built personal brands and companies themselves, and they are excellent touchpoints for you as you rehab your own career.

I will also share my personal success story: I was an unhappy employee who rebranded my technology career, which helped me land enjoyable six-figure jobs. Some of these roles were 100 percent remote, which means I never went into the office. Within the past ten years, I have rehabbed my career by rebranding my resume, identifying a reasonable commute, and enhancing my career-development skills. I have since been able to call the shots for my career. I have interviewed with companies like Deloitte Consulting, Microsoft, and tech startups and converted my career-rehab success into a strong brand that allowed me to be featured in Glassdoor, Yahoo!, CNN, *The Washington Post*, and Entrepreneur.com, and on many podcasts.

Most important, you will read about how to take actionable steps to rehab your career. In this digital age, there is no need for you to stay in a job you don't like and be underpaid. This book will outline innovative ways and simple methods you can use to brand, market, and sell yourself into jobs that promote work-life balance, fair compensation, and continuous career development. The collection of research, clients' success stories, interviews, and case studies will give you a better understanding of how career rehab can enhance your professional happiness and leverage your personal passions and purpose in life. It's time to strip away what no longer works.

1

WHAT IS CAREER REHAB?

Career rehab is both a state of mind and a plan of action designed to help you restore and renew your career. In simple terms, career rehab is taking control of your career and remaining resilient amidst poor career experiences. It enhances your ability to cope even when you dislike your co-workers, work assignments, management team, commute, compensation, or some other aspect of your job.

In the introduction, I used the analogy that career rehab is like building or renovating a home: Sometimes you have to tear it down and rebuild it from a new foundation before you can brand, market, and sell it. It's perfectly OK that you may have to start from ground zero as you build or rebuild your personal brand. You are not just an employee—you are a product that offers a unique skill set to an organization. All major businesses go through product-development phases before they launch a new product, and it's no different with your career development. Products are designed, built, tested, and launched. We will take the same approach with your career. You will learn how to create the career you want by designing, building, testing, and launching your personal brand through my Rehab YOU process. In this chapter, I will walk you through the major stages of career rehab so you can prepare to take stock of your career, create a blueprint for success, and take the action steps you need to turn your "fixer-upper" career into the career of your dreams.

Rehab YOU

Rehab YOU is a framework I created to assist professionals in rehabbing their careers. It will help you design how your career will look, first by creating new ideas for your career path and professional goals. Next you will build your personal brand by creating the foundation with your education, experience, and expertise. Then you will test your personal brand by putting out your resume on LinkedIn and other job board websites. Finally you will launch your revamped personal brand and sell it as you attend hiring events and land job interviews. The phases of the framework look like this:

→ Design (Ideation)
→ Build (Branding)
→ Test (Marketing)
→ Launch (Selling)

This framework is your master plan for rehab. They are not hard and fast steps but rather a general guide as you make the moves you need to create your personal brand that will take your career to the next level, from diagnosing your career issues to creating a career blueprint. Let's take a quick look at the main pieces of this framework.

Idea

The idea phase of Rehab YOU is a simple one—brainstorm! Think about all the potential career paths and goals you have for yourself and how those might intersect. Nothing is out of bounds at this point, so get creative. What paths might you take? What do you really want out of your professional life?

Brand

The art of creating your personal brand will require you to identify key technical skills and soft skills that you will need as you identify what industry you want to go into. You will create a personal brand that will go beyond your resume and LinkedIn profile. You will become an industry expert in your field; you will back up your personal brand with education, professional certifications, internships, online portfolios, blogs, white papers and presentations, etc.

Market

As you become an industry expert, you have to market your knowledge, skills, and experience using a strategic marketing plan specific to your career goals. To do that, you will need to create an online brand presence on social media and a solid resume that will get noticed by hiring managers.

Sell

To sell yourself as a personal brand, you need to network like a hustler and sell yourself at meetups, conferences, and hiring events, which can help industry leaders know you exist. You also need to learn how to be yourself and sell yourself in your job interviews and interactions with recruiters and industry leaders.

The Diagnosis

The process of diagnosing your career is not unlike when a contractor assesses your home for repair or restoration. Take the time to evaluate yourself and your career and decide what career path is right for you, based on the Rehab YOU framework. Career assessments are a great way to help you understand what education, experience, and exposure you need to take your career to the next level. An assessment will aid you in identifying your strengths, weaknesses, and interests for that new job you may wish to apply for or that career change you may desire to pursue. You may need a full career makeover or only a few minor enhancements, but either way the assessment will help you decide your next steps.

I have created a "Rehab YOU Evaluation" so you can put the pieces of your career back together for that career change, new promotion, or new entry into the work force. This diagnosis will help you identify which career path you are on: the cool geek, the corporate rebel, or the career dropout. You will learn how to evaluate and rehab your career for your current career path and gain a clearer understanding of what career option is the best fit as you Rehab YOU.

Reposition Yourself

Before we dive deep into rehabbing your career, we should take a step back and deal with a tough topic: depression and anxiety. Jobs that you don't like or that feel overwhelming can cause depression and anxiety. According to the career-development website Monster, depression and anxiety can seriously affect your performance at work. In a 2006 survey by the Anxiety and Depression Association of America (ADAA), 56 percent of respondents said their stress and anxiety levels affected their workplace performance, 51 percent said it had a negative impact on their relationship with their co-workers and peers, 50 percent said it affected the quality of their work, and 43 percent pointed to their relationships with superiors. Career mental illness is not always a topic career coaches and HR experts address, but in this book, I will provide researched methods and coping mechanisms for dealing with stress on the job, surviving bad leadership, and staying in a job you are not passionate about so you can reposition yourself for success.

The Rehab YOU Career Blueprint

One of the most important phases of your career rehab journey is creating your Rehab YOU career blueprint. When an architect builds a home, the blueprint clearly lays out its specifications. As you "rehab you" for your career goals, keep in mind the four phases of the Rehab YOU framework (design, build, test, and launch) to determine what you want your renovated career to look like. Become the architect of your career by considering your desired career path, location, salary, scope, organization type, benefits and perks, and mentors. Throughout the Rehab YOU process, you will start to feel more confident in your career renovations as you craft your vision of your dream career.

Be a Brand, Not an Employee

Once you have your blueprint in place, you can start taking actionable steps to rehab your career, starting with your personal brand. Most employees don't see themselves as brands because they don't feel empowered by their company's leadership or they don't like what they do every day. As you rehab your career, you will identify your strengths, subject-matter expertise, and professional experience and use those to create your brand. You will also learn a new mindset to help see yourself as a brand, not just an employee, by working on special projects, giving presentations, and writing white papers.

One way to do that is to create your own sense of empowerment—even when you crave feedback from others. According to the 2014 "Workplace Accountability Study" by management consulting firm Partners in Leadership, 80 percent of respondents said they only receive feedback when they make a mistake or perform poorly. How is that empowering? Such feedback makes employees feel shamed and stuck in their jobs. The brand mindset, however, helps professionals feel empowered whether they do well or poorly. The empowerment of your personal brand comes with having confidence in your skills, experience, and training. Career rehab will help you feel empowered to create an epic career for yourself when you are performing well—and help you learn from your mistakes when you aren't.

Build Your Brand by "Dating" Jobs

As a professional career coach, I always advise my clients who have landed jobs at companies like Bank of America, Capital One, and Microsoft that it's healthy to "date" jobs until you find the one you love. In other words, don't be afraid to try a job for a limited time and then move on; it's OK to find a new job every 12 to 24 months. The more professional experience you have, the more you learn and the more you can earn. The career rehab journey does not encourage you to stay in a job you hate. Remember: You tolerate the job—it does not tolerate you. Not only do you build your personal brand as you date jobs, but you are constantly building your professional network as well. My motto is: Date jobs and marry the dream. Until you find your dream job, define your purpose, and execute your passions, you should date jobs before settling down.

Market Yourself Like an Ad

As you date jobs and develop your personal brand, learn how to market your new experience and skills using social media. As you read earlier, the third phase in the Rehab YOU process is called "test," which means you will use social media, websites, and job boards to market yourself like a product. Some of the best authors, speakers, actors, and athletes use the internet to market their personal brands. You will learn how to socialize your brand by using your resume and LinkedIn profile and by connecting with other professionals in online groups and forums. The world needs to know you exist.

Be You, Sell You

As you market yourself and test what works, you need to get ready to launch your personal brand by focusing on authenticity. You will soon be selling yourself to industry leaders, recruiters, and hiring managers, so the real question is: What are you selling to them besides your resume? Where is the real you?

You will learn how to launch your brand by selling yourself through presentations, blogs, websites, white papers, and courses that will enhance people's perception of your professional experience, and you will become more comfortable with selling your authentic self by going to job interviews, speaking at conferences, attending meetups, and participating in networking events.

Network Like a Hustler

Networking is a critical asset to rebuilding your personal brand. Professional networking is not easy for everyone since we all have different personalities. Some of us are introverts and others are extroverts, but no matter what your personality type is you will be able to expand your network once you understand all the career benefits of professional networking. You will have better understanding of how you can adopt a hustler's mindset and network in person and online.

You will learn how to how to network online using social media, virtual events, and online learning platforms. Also, you will learn how to network in person within the workplace, professional events, personal/social events, and at colleges/educational environments. Professional networking expands your industry knowledge as you learn from others and it opens doors to new career opportunities.

Get Paid Now: Money, Power, and Respect

No one wants to go through the process of designing, building, testing, and launching their revamped personal brand without getting the pay, power, and respect they deserve along with their new role. This piece of the career rehab process will teach you how to negotiate your salary, benefits, and incentives using the professional experience and education you already have. That sounds easy, but most professionals don't take the time to research the correct salary range for their city and state, leaving them at a disadvantage when negotiating. It's time to take back your power. Don't rehab your career only to take pennies or look desperate as you launch your job search. Later in the book, I will share how my clients landed six-figure salaries with telecommuting options. I will also discuss how women, minorities, and retirees can get the pay they deserve, since historically that population of professionals has been undervalued and underpaid.

Break Up with Jobs: Fearless Resignations

At this stage in your career rehab journey, you may be getting job offers, and you may even be ready to accept one of them. Once you do, you will need to know how to properly and fearlessly resign from your current job, and HR experts and I are here to show you how.

I like to call it "breaking up" with jobs. Since you will be dating jobs, you will always have to break up with a job for a new role that is a better fit for your career rehab goals and personal brand. You will learn how to create a professional resignation letter, properly transition your existing tasks to other employees, and leave on a positive note.

Don't Overcommit to Work

The career rehab journey is all about letting go of what doesn't work for you and deciding how your career should be renovated, developed, and managed. Your career should always be centered around work-life balance. I think we all have experienced working a job that was stressful or demanded more than 40 hours per week. But rehabbing your career will help you understand new ways to eat right, exercise, spend time with your family, and take vacations. This chapter will help you put your physical, mental, and spiritual well-being first while still having an awesome career.

Commutes Worth the Coins

I live in Washington, DC, and our metropolitan area is ranked as having the longest average car commute: 43.6 minutes, according to 2016 U.S. Census Bureau data. The average one-way commute in the U.S., per the same source, is 26.1 minutes. That adds up to 4.35 hours a week and more than 200 hours (nearly nine days) per year for full-time employees. In my experience as a career coach, professionals who have a long commute tend not to have great work-life balance and are not as excited about their jobs as someone with a commute under 30 minutes. But that's not going to be you. You are going to execute a job search strategy that gives you more career opportunities close to home and provides telecommuting options throughout the week.

Life After Retirement

I know what you've been thinking: When are we going to talk about the retirees? As you read earlier, I like to call retirees career dropouts, because they have worked for 30 years or more, and they may be ready to never work again. They are done with employment as usual, but they may be ready to volunteer their time or start a new business. According to the AARP, some retirees still want to work part time for contract positions, and working 20 hours a week gives them more financial security. They use the income as "fun money" to take vacations and pay off small bills. I have interviewed retirees who have done all three: volunteered, started a business, and launched a new career. Their career rehab journey has led them to happiness, focusing on new career goals, mapping out their finances, and launching their business ideas.

Divorce the Job for the Dream

Career rehabbers can win big by landing awesome jobs, but some have a passion for creating a business. They want to make something that is theirs alone. You may follow a similar path: As you date many jobs and find one you love, there may still come a day when you want to divorce that job and marry your dream of entrepreneurship, even if you feel scared about leaving your comfortable job to start a business. You can prepare for this new milestone with confidence, though. You have to rehab a business idea the same way you rehab a career: by designing, building, testing, and launching your new product or service. You will learn how to plan financially, create the business while you are still working, and find investors and clients before the career divorce is final.

Stay Focused on YOU

Career rehab takes a lot of work. But the most difficult part is maintaining a healthy career lifestyle and solid personal brand as you do it. It can be hard to sustain a good work-life balance, a healthy lifestyle, and a good working relationship with the jobs you date. We have to care for ourselves, our families, and our careers without falling into patterns of neglect that can tear away at the "good bones" of our careers. Career rehab is not a one-time renovation but a lifestyle, and I will give you practical ways to maintain the personal brand you are building as you deal with the ups and downs of life. You will also learn how to update your online brand, resume, technical skills, and professional experience as you advance in your current job and as you break up with jobs for new roles. So let's dive right in and take a look at what is going on in your career "house."

☆ Meet Malcolm Thomas, IT Cool Geek

Malcolm Thomas is a database administrator. His expertise is primarily focused on the Extract, Transform, and Load (ETL) process. He works with a nonprofit organization that is the operational hub of satellite locations providing services such as marketing, branding, business development, and analytics.

Malcolm Thomas, continued

⭐ What did your career looked like before you started your career in information technology?

⭐ Before IT, I was an aviation mechanic in the U.S. Military. I had no intentions on transitioning to IT. I was considered a subject-matter expert in aviation and had a very promising career. During that career, I was selected for every promotion immediately. After nine years of service, I separated from the military to be present in my family's lives. From there, I relocated my family to the metro Atlanta area. I quickly learned that the workforce required me to have a degree in any field in order to gain a new position. So I went from being a professional to a student. For one year, I studied electrical engineering before relocating to the Washington, DC metro area. There I became a professional security officer as a stop gap until completing my education. While being in the new area, I saw many opportunities to enter the IT field. This propelled me to change my blueprint.

⭐ What steps did you take to develop your career blueprint for the information technology field?

⭐ In the Washington, DC metro area I quickly realized that a degree in electrical engineering would not be advantageous. Based on my research, IT had the most potential in this area in terms of experience level required to enter the industry, longevity, and advancement. I knew to change my degree plan from electrical engineering to IT; however, I had no clue towards what branch of IT would best suit me. With the help of my academic advisors and my own research, I decided that database administration was similar to the things I like to do. So I enrolled in the University of Phoenix associate's program in information technology with a focus in database administration. Ultimately, my exact steps to develop my career were to identify what I wanted to do, analyze what steps I needed to take, manage my time effectively, implement controls to keep me on my path, and supervise my roadmap until completion.

⭐ Do you think career builders like career coaches, mentors, and managers have helped you advance in your career?

⭐ Absolutely! I spent countless hours thinking that I knew what to do to get a job. For the three years after separating from the military, I was only afforded one opportunity

Malcolm Thomas, continued

to earn income after many application submissions. Clearly I had no clue what I was doing. I used the advisors at the University of Phoenix during school to assist in entering IT, which helped me build a network with alumni. After school, expectations were high, but I had no luck in finding any leads to IT. I used my own devices for many months, and still no luck. Through the process, I was introduced to you by a mutual colleague. Meeting with you literally accelerated my process in finding my new career. You showed me techniques to optimize job searches and write a resume that allowed me to showcase skills that grabbed the attention of IT recruiters while still being authentically me.

⭐ *What advice would you give to someone who has no career blueprint and does not know where to start?*

⭐ Find a career coach who has the skills and expertise related to your industry. The road to landing a good job and starting a new career can be tricky, and arduous, and should never be navigated alone. No matter your experience level, education, or work history, there is a special technique to finding a job. It is not as easy as hopping on a job search engine and clicking "Apply." What I now know relating to creating a personal blueprint for career advancement is owed to the professionals who help everyday people find new careers.

2

CAREER REHAB: THE DIAGNOSIS

Most professionals who hate their jobs feel the symptoms mentally or physically every day they report to work. Their feelings appear in their attitudes toward their daily tasks, team members, leadership, commute, and lack of opportunity. Reflecting on your reality at work is the first step toward identifying how you truly feel about your job and deciding whether you need to rehab your career. These honest reflections also dictate whether you need to do a Rehab YOU evaluation for your entire personal brand, which I'll cover later in this chapter.

To begin, think about your day-to-day work life. Do you identify with the following symptoms? If so, it might be time for a career rehab. Ask yourself if any of the following ten statements are true:

1. There is no professional development or job promotion potential at your place of work.
2. Your passion for the job does not exist.
3. You don't like going to work; you have a negative attitude.
4. The workload causes you stress and depression.
5. Your leadership and team members are difficult to work with.
6. Your commute is too long and is affecting your work-life balance.
7. You feel stuck due to your limited experience, education, and skills.
8. Your job is affecting your relationship with your family.
9. You feel insecure about networking and interviewing for new jobs.
10. Your resume is not getting noticed by recruiters online.

If any of these speak to you, you're ready to drill down into a more specific self-diagnosis. In this chapter, we'll cover some simple diagnostics you can perform on your own to help identify what parts of your career brand need a little renovation.

Diagnose Yourself

Once you decide that you need career rehab, it's time to evaluate the state of your career and determine which program is a good fit for your personal career brand. This is the "diagnosis" phase. It's similar to a contractor inspecting a home they're planning to renovate: You're going to evaluate what remains strong, what could use some minor repairs, and what needs to be completely gutted and rebuilt. This inspection of your career is called the Rehab YOU Evaluation. This evaluation will require you to be transparent and open to new ways of designing, building, testing, and launching your personal brand, once you select the career path that is right for you.

The concept of the Rehab YOU Evaluation is deeply rooted in my own experience as a professional, when I had to do the hard work of assessing my path. When I was working in the federal government, I was deeply unhappy for more than five years. I had to evaluate my current career state and determine if that version of my personal brand was worth saving, needed updating, or would have to be rebuilt altogether. I had to develop a plan for my new IT career path in the private sector, while being honest with myself about the skills I had to learn and the IT certifications I needed to transition into a role as a senior consultant to Fortune 500 companies (which is where I ultimately wanted to end up). I had to shift my mindset and learn to be brave as I did some serious self-reflection. In short, I had to level up my career to match the brand I wanted to create. The Rehab YOU Evaluation is the first step in accepting that you, too, may need to level up your career.

The Rehab YOU Evaluation is a full walk-through of your current career state. It can help you develop robust and scalable ways to build or rebuild your personal brand for that first job out of college, new promotion, or career change. You can then reuse this evaluation as you advance in your career or change your career path. Whether you are a recent college graduate, current professional, or retiree, this evaluation will identify how to move forward as you Rehab YOU. Let's get started!

The Rehab YOU Evaluation

When I decided to rehab my own career back in 2014, I went out and bought unlined journals and sketchbooks. If I was going to embrace this evaluation process, I wanted to draw pictures, scribble down ideas, and create to-do lists with no boundaries. I felt stuck in my career, and it was time to do a full inspection. So to get started, pick up an inexpensive sketchbook or journal along with whatever kind of writing instruments you like (pencils, pens, highlighters, markers—whatever sparks your creativity). Then start digging into the various aspects of your career by answering the questions in the following sections, which align with the four parts of the Rehab YOU framework you first read about in Chapter 1.

Design (Ideation)

Brainstorm what you want your career path to look like and the lifestyle that will bring you happiness. Be creative—your career path can include nontraditional ideas or linear moves up your current job ladder. No matter what, though, design a career that feels right for you and aligns with the things you enjoy doing. Ask yourself these two questions:

1. Do you have a defined career path? If so, what does it look like?
2. Is your current career path bringing you happiness? If not, what career path would you like to pursue? Describe a career path that aligns with your passions or purpose.

The process of designing your career path helps map out your career blueprint. If you don't have a career blueprint that is aligned with your goals and passions, it's time to renovate!

Build (Branding)

Identify what education, skills, certifications, training, and professional experience you will need to build your personal brand. As you build your brand, think about what soft skills you will need to work on the types of projects that will help you grow in your career path. Too often, professionals focus on necessary technical skills and forget about the communication, writing, and presentation skills they will need to enhance their personal brand. Ask yourself these two questions:

1. What formal education (college degrees, certifications, training) do you have or need for your career path?
2. Do you need more education, skills, or professional experience to accomplish your career goals for your chosen path?

If you lack the formal education that you need for your career path, you cannot build the foundation of your personal brand. You don't always need a college degree to get the new role that you desire. Sometimes you just need a training course or certifications. The more technical certifications and courses you take, the more money you can demand. The Global Knowledge 2019 IT Skills and Salary Report says that the highest-paying certifications emphasize hard skills like cloud computing and cybersecurity and people skills like networking and project management.

Test (Marketing)

Test the career marketplace by creating a profile on LinkedIn and placing your resume on the most popular job board sites; this will help get you noticed by recruiters. As you market yourself, make sure you have the right buzzwords in your resume so recruiters can find you online. Ask yourself the following two questions:

1. Does your current resume align with your desired career path?
2. Have you created a LinkedIn profile and online job board profiles?

If your current resume does not align with your career goals, you will find it very difficult to test your personal brand as you market yourself on LinkedIn and job board sites like Indeed.com and Monster.com. You will need to rehab your resume before you start marketing yourself for your dream job.

Launch (Selling)

Sell your authentic self in job interviews, networking events, meetups, and conferences. When you relaunch your personal brand, you want to have top-notch networking and interview skills as you present yourself to recruiters, hiring managers, and fellow professionals. The art of selling yourself requires you to become comfortable introducing your personal brand to people who can help you land the job you desire. Ask yourself two questions:

1. Do you feel comfortable getting ready for job interviews? Do you perform well in interviews?

2. Do you attend networking events, hiring events, and conferences to connect with like-minded professional leaders, recruiters, and hiring managers?

If you need to improve your interview skills and you don't currently attend events where you can sell your professional experience and education, you need career rehab.

Career Rehab Paths

Next, you can identify what career rehab path you are on. Each path aligns with where you are in your career journey. Wherever you are, Rehab YOU is a reusable process that will come in handy as you evolve in your career from college, through corporate life, and into entrepreneurship, so you can always return for another round of renovations.

Since I have undergone career rehab myself (and coached others through the process), I have created these categories for my clients to help them tailor their personal-branding needs. The following career rehab paths align with your career tenure, professional experience, and goals. As we move through the career rehab program, I will repeatedly return to these three paths/personas to showcase how these concepts can apply to you no matter where you are in your journey.

Cool Geeks

Cool geeks are typically recent high school or college graduates with less than five years of professional work experience. They are looking to align their formal education with organizations that will help them build their professional experience through internships, entry-level positions, and volunteer opportunities.

WHAT WILL YOU LEARN?

If you are a cool geek, career rehab will help speed up the process of finding a job that matches your degree. Too often, many graduates have a hard time finding a job they like that aligns with their education or formal training. You will learn how to apply to internships, build a resume that stands out, and get comfortable with selling yourself in job interviews. This program will teach you the fundamentals of personal branding that will help you advance fast in the first five years of your career. You will learn how to find career happiness early and how to "date" jobs while you are an intern so you can find the perfect match while the stakes are lower.

Corporate Rebels

These are professionals with more than five years of experience who are ready to level up their career with a promotion or new job. Corporate rebels are ready to go against the grain. They may have experienced career heartbreaks, or they may simply be ready to learn and earn more with their current career path.

WHAT WILL YOU LEARN?

If you are a corporate rebel, career rehab will help you maximize your professional worth within your current career path. You will identify the skills and certifications you need to qualify for new roles that pay close to or beyond your salary goals. You will also learn how to level up your resume, spruce up your LinkedIn profile and job board accounts, and highlight new skills that will get you noticed by recruiters. You will be rehabbing your career for limitless advancement and learning to sell yourself like an enhanced product.

Career Dropouts

Career dropouts are professionals who want a career change. They are ready for a new career path that will make them happy. They may also be retirees (or almost retirees) who are thinking of starting a new career in their retirement years.

WHAT WILL YOU LEARN?

This program is designed to help you learn how to build your new career or business by leveraging your current education, experience, and skills. Identifying what is transferable will help you design, build, test, and launch your new career path. This program will also help you identify what education, training, and skills you need to succeed in your new journey. The idea of rehab is to gut what you don't need and add value to what you already have. As you work a nine-to-five or retirement gig, you will learn how to create a business that offers products and services to the right consumers and clients.

Keep an Open Mind

As you embark on this career rehab journey, it can feel a little overwhelming, confusing, and even scary. All those emotions are normal during the diagnosis process, but once you begin to renovate your career, it will start to feel good. As you put the first building blocks of your career together, you will feel a few steps nearer to a career that will bring you more happiness and less stress. The Rehab YOU framework will require some work, but it will be fun work that brings you closer to your epic future.

Rehab YOU Checklist

The Rehab YOU checklist is an easy way to make sure your personal brand is on the right track. At times you may feel overwhelmed, but this ten-item checklist will help you understand how to rehab your career with the right actions, tools, and commitment.

- ❏ Think about your career rehab reflections. How is your career currently making you feel?
- ❏ Purchase a career rehab journal and complete the Rehab YOU self-evaluation.
- ❏ Write down or sketch out your career goals and passions. This will help you DESIGN your personal brand.
- ❏ Write down or sketch out the education, skills, certifications, training, and professional experience you will need to build your personal brand. This will help you BUILD your personal brand.

❏ Write down or sketch out where you can add your resume online or how you will begin to enhance your LinkedIn profile to help you TEST your personal brand.

❏ Write down or sketch out a list of conferences, meetups, or hiring events you want to attend. This will help you LAUNCH your revamped personal brand in the future.

❏ Select a career rehab coaching program that will help Rehab YOU.

❏ Be patient with the process. There is so much to learn, unpack, and pack into your new personal brand.

❏ Keep an open mindset and a brave heart as you move forward on this journey.

❏ Begin your career rehab journey today!

The Rehab YOU checklist is a great way to ensure that you are on the right track to designing, building, testing, and launching your personal brand. Personal-brand development requires some vetting while you are in career rehab. Vetting your personal brand against this checklist is a great way to assess what is working and what is not.

☆ Meet Courteney Crawley-Dyson, Marketing Cool Geek

Courteney Crawley-Dyson is one of my coaching clients. She works as a marketing assistant in Maryland, where she maintains the production of digital and print materials. She is also the sole proprietor of her own business, The Kairos Graphics Designs, a graphic design service in metro Washington, DC. Her professional knowledge encompasses competitive marketing techniques, social media strategic planning, and visual communications. Her journey helps showcase the importance of having a career rehab plan of action.

☆ *Explain what your career looked like before you created an online portfolio, resume, and LinkedIn profile.*

Courteney Crawley-Dyson, continued

⭐ Before my LinkedIn platform was created, I earned minimum-wage income as a part-time sales representative for Crate & Barrel. This job provided me the social impact necessary for professional development; however, leadership promotions were difficult for me to obtain, and it created an extremely unmotivated environment for me. I graduated with an Associate of Arts degree in general education in 2018 and worked a dead-end, part-time job for a company that did not fulfill my career aspirations. Despite the hopeless outlook of my prior job, work opportunities poured in once I took the initiative to apply myself as a true motivated professional to career organizations.

⭐ *What steps did you take to develop your graphics design portfolio and company website?*

⭐ My graphic design portfolio and public website developed with professional engagement and volunteer performance. Once the volunteer work took off, I advanced my efforts with paid clientele and created a clean online portfolio. The work showcased my projects in collaboration with Blue Knights LEMC Maryland Chapter 1, Overseas Private Investment Corp., and the We Are All Educators Org., to name a few.

⭐ *What online tools do you use to market your education, experience, and expertise?*

⭐ I am familiar with Adobe and Microsoft software, as well as other social media platforms used for curating research, designs, and implementation of market plans. In my efforts to maintain prevailing knowledge, I constantly learned from online learning platforms.

⭐ *What type of success, job interviews, and job offers have you experienced since you started marketing your online work?*

⭐ Since my online personal brand marketing began, I have professionally interviewed with WETA-TV, received job offers from Amazon, and published with the United States government's development finance institution, my alumni high school's educator's program, and with the Maryland-National Capital Park and Planning Commission. All of these are prideful successes that follow hard work and dedication to achieving my goals and working with excellent people who believe in making job experiences a dream come true.

☆ ☆ ☆

REPOSITION YOURSELF

O nce you have assessed where you are and what steps you want to take to rehab your career, it's time to deal with any bad emotions and attitudes you may have toward your past or current jobs. You can't Rehab YOU if you're carrying depression, anxiety, and stress along with you. The career rehab process should be fun and offer you an exciting outlook on what is to come as you go after your career goals. It should not be a time to wallow in negativity about your past choices. Career coaches spend a lot of time teaching about personal branding, but sometimes we forget that our clients are human, and their personal and professional challenges (like feeling depressed or overwhelmed after a job change or loss) can cause them to shut down emotionally. So before we get too deep into your career rehab journey, I want you to understand how to address your personal and career-related challenges and set yourself up for future success. In other words, it's time to reposition yourself for success.

Rethink Stress

The adverse effects of being unhappy in their job can be very painful for professionals who really want to see a way out of dealing with a bad manager, a toxic workplace, or even just a job they are not passionate about. Or your stress, anxiety, and depression may be the result of a personal issue, and it may become hard to perform well on the job and communicate with your leadership team. These personal and professional pressures can lead to conflicts at home and on the job. Ultimately, stress makes it hard to see a path forward.

It's important to know that you are not alone. According to a 2018 Gallup Poll, 55 percent of those surveyed said they experience stress during much of the day, and 45 percent said they feel worried often.

Stress and anxiety disorders are damaging professionals' work life and their relationships with their children and spouses. Coping with these disorders can be very difficult (especially if you lack support, either at home or through your health-care system), and not all companies are transparent about these issues. Some managers just want the work done even if the workload is unrealistic, and they still want quality work despite a lack of resources. It can be an untenable situation.

Some people think anxiety and depression are a sign of weakness, but within the career rehab process, I like to look at them as strengths: Think of them as a launching pad you can use to get your career on the right track. Anxiety and stress are a sign that you care about your life and career, which is a good thing. You just have to learn new ways to channel your emotions into actions that will help you cope instead of spending most of your time worrying about what is causing you to feel so bad in the first place. It's all about flipping the stress script.

Flip the Stress Script

Job stress has varying sources and multiple professional and personal consequences, according to the ADAA in its landmark 2006 survey on workplace stress.

The survey cites the main sources of job-related stress as:

→ deadlines (55 percent)
→ interpersonal relationships (53 percent)
→ staff management (50 percent)
→ dealing with issues/problems that arise (49 percent)

Employees report that stress and anxiety regularly affects:

→ workplace performance (56 percent)
→ relationship with co-workers and peers (51 percent)
→ quality of work (50 percent)
→ relationships with superiors (43 percent)

These results are in line with comments I hear from clients, and the main take-away I offer them is this: You have to turn those negatives into positives so you can reposition your career journey, and that starts with addressing stress. The best way to reduce your workplace stress is to beware of your stress triggers. You have to be clear about what sets the tone for your emotions and thoughts when stress attacks your state of mind at work. Most professionals ignore their triggers and never try to find new ways to cope. The stress becomes their normal way of life. Despite the stress you deal with on a regular basis, you need to learn how to take that energy and use it to promote your career accomplishments, milestones, and expertise. Here are some examples:

→ When you learn how to complete your workload with very few resources or support from leadership, even though the experience may be stressful, that is a strength another organization will value.

→ When you can effectively communicate in person and writing with difficult team members and stakeholders, you can take that ability to a company that has a more positive culture.

→ When you overcome stressful situations, you are the real MVP, and there is a company out there looking for hardworking team players and future leaders like you.

Take these stressful experiences and reverse them into success stories for your personal brand. The best brands tell stories of winning against all odds. Professional obstacles make our skills stronger—use that to your advantage.

Ten Ways to Reverse Your Workplace Stress into Success

Here are some tactical ideas for turning workplace stress into success, even when you are faced with what seem like overwhelming situations. Try these tips:

1. Write down your workplace stressors in a journal.
2. Create new ways to respond to your stress that will help you remain calm.
3. Find a quiet place where you can meditate or pray daily.
4. Take frequent breaks at work when your workload is heavy.
5. When you go home in the evenings and on weekends, learn how to chill out and get some rest.
6. Work out a few times per week. Cardio and weightlifting will help you release stress.
7. Eat foods that are healthy for your brain and promote energy: veggies, fruit, lean protein, and water.
8. Spend time with your family: It often helps you keep things in perspective.
9. Try to take time off or work from home to relieve personal stressors.
10. Communicate with your supervisor when your workload is too heavy.

Stress, anxiety, and depression are like mold in a house that needs to be rehabbed. You have to eliminate it because it's toxic, and it can harm you or even kill you. It's the same thing with your career. You cannot allow stress, anxiety, and depression to ruin your career goals and dreams. One way to do that is to stop being career SAD.

Stop Being Career SAD

I know it's hard to always be happy about your current job situation. Career sadness can build over years and affect your confidence, but you have to gut the sadness out and get to the root of what will make you happy. We all have a core that embodies our gifts, passions, and expertise, leading us to a path of career happiness. The process of letting go of this sadness will require you to fight off the mental, physical, and spiritual side effects of stress, anxiety, and depression.

Your career rehab process deserves a HAPPY mindset. You can't Rehab YOU feeling:

Stress
Anxiety
Depression

So let's lose the SAD. We are going to rename SAD to ADS (short for advertisements), because as you build your personal brand, you will be a walking advertisement for the industry you want to work in. You have to turn your SAD into ADS as you brand, market, and sell yourself.

Marketers judge ads by how successful they are at selling products and services. Professionals are human ads, and we use our education and experience to determine our own success by selling our personal brands through our resumes, LinkedIn profiles, and job-board websites. For the career rehab process, this is how we'll break down the ADS approach:

Accomplish. Turn your anxiety into accomplishments.

+

Dominate. Make your depression take a back seat to success.

=

Success. Enjoy the results of flipping the script on sadness, anxiety, and depression.

This is how to reframe your ideas about stress and reposition them into benefits for your career rehab journey. Let's look at the two main steps (Accomplish plus Dominating) that will help you reach the Success stage.

Step 1: Turn Anxiety into Accomplishments

Stress sometimes triggers anxieties about work. It's interesting how they work together to cripple your job performance. The uphill battle of turning your anxiety into accomplishments resides in the fact that most of us don't know how to manage our stress levels, which gives us anxiety resulting in fear. For professionals, fear of the unknown may be what their manager will think of them, or whether they will complete a task on time. Some professionals fear networking, social engagement, and job interviews. Anxiety-driven fear makes you feel like you can't accomplish what you set out to do. This fear will delay your career rehab process because you won't feel confident in your ability to level up your career. You have to replace that fear with faith. Faith will help you design, build, test, and launch your career and land your dream job. Once you make it through the process, you will see there was never anything to fear. Workplace anxiety is very common, but finding a welcoming work culture with a supportive team and manager can help ease some of that fear of failure.

Over time, these workplace anxiety attacks can turn into disorders for some professionals, including panic disorder, social anxiety disorder, generalized anxiety disorder, and even specific fears and phobias.

According to the CBHS Health Fund, some typical workplace anxieties may include:

- → Fear of public speaking or sharing in meetings
- → Fear of working in groups
- → Fear of deadlines
- → Worrying about one's quality of work
- → Fear of being judged by coworkers
- → Fear of humiliation

→ Fear of interacting with authority figures

→ Fear associated with requesting a promotion

So how do you combat these anxieties so they can instead benefit your career rehab journey? Here are ten ways to turn your anxiety into accomplishments:

1. Create a daily to-do list and prioritize your tasks in small chunks or microgoals.

2. Develop an honest and transparent relationship with your supervisor.

3. Build relationships with professionals on your team who can help you when you run into trouble with a complex task.

4. Communicate in person when you need clarity on a deliverable; sometimes emails and phone calls don't help you progress.

5. Don't get involved in office politics or drama; it will only increase your fear and anxiety.

6. Set realistic and concise deadlines, and don't overcommit when you are assigned a task.

7. Update your team members and manager weekly on your progress, so if the deadline needs to be extended, they will have been involved the entire time.

8. Identify what calms you down when you are working. Maybe listening to music or working alone in a conference room can create a new sense of peace for you.

9. Get more sleep at night; being better-rested will help you feel less anxious.

10. Talk your feelings out with someone who understands your anxiety attacks. A sympathetic listener will help calm you down when they strike.

The battle of anxiety can be difficult; it takes practice and self-awareness to cope on a regular basis. You will not win every fight, but each time you conquer an attack, it makes the next one easier to handle. The key is to focus on the small victories, assess your reactions, and keep trying to react more positively each time.

Step 2: Dominate Your Depression

Career and/or personal depression may have affected you at some time in your life. But creating a lifestyle that can help you cope with depression is vital to the process of dominating it. When you feel depressed, you don't feel like you can accomplish anything. The simplest tasks, like getting out of bed or going to work, can seem daunting. Sometimes it may be hard for you to tackle your assignments at work or feel empowered to level up your career. The negative thoughts and feelings you experience during depression may make you cut yourself off from family and friends. Isolation is a key sign of depression for people who are suffering from the death of a loved one, a tough financial situation, or a bad relationship.

According to the American Psychiatric Association (APA), depression symptoms can vary from mild to severe and can include:

- → Feelings of sadness or depressed mood
- → Loss of interest or pleasure in activities
- → Changes in appetite
- → Trouble sleeping
- → Loss of energy
- → Difficulty concentrating
- → Thoughts of death or suicide

Any or all of these symptoms may indicate that you are experiencing depression, which may significantly impact your career. When depression hits you, it can be hard to even think about rehabbing your personal brand. It may be the *last* thing you are thinking about; you just feel hopeless. But the great thing about career rehab is that it can help you better manage your sadness by moving your focus from how you feel to how you *want* to feel.

Here are four key steps you can take to overcome feelings of depression and refocus your mindset in your personal life:

1. *Stay connected with those who truly love and care about you.* Don't just pick up the phone and call. It's very healthy to have face-to-face conversations about how you are feeling.

2. *Talk to a therapist.* There is nothing wrong with seeking professional help. If you are suffering from depression, working with a therapist will help you develop new coping mechanisms.

3. *Identify fun activities you love to do.* Attempting to do the things you love will help you manage your depression.

4. *Avoid illegal drugs and alcohol.* They only suppress your feelings of depression and can actually worsen them. The use of drugs and alcohol when you are depressed can easily lead to addiction, creating further problems.

All that said, depression isn't something you only address outside work. You have to address how it affects you in the office as well. When depression is caused by job-related circumstances, it can be very hard to navigate work-performance challenges and healthy working relationships with your co-workers and management team. There is no worse feeling than being physically at work while your mind is somewhere else due to depression. It's like you are a zombie. And yet you have to keep coming to work because you have bills to pay.

Here are six ways to tackle depression at work:

1. *Find out if your company offers confidential counseling programs.* Most large organizations offer free counseling to their employees. You can work with your HR department or employee relations department to find out what your company offers.

2. *Take frequent breaks at work.* It's OK to take a walk outside and enjoy the sunshine, which can bring a little more joy into your life when you are trying to manage your symptoms of depression.

3. *Make your cubicle or office feel more like you.* Place pictures of your family on your desk. Hang artwork or funny quotes on the wall that can make you smile in your times of depression at work.

4. *Find someone on your team whom you can exercise with during lunch or after work.* A workout buddy is great for

accountability, and it will also allow you to work off those feelings of sadness.

5. *Go to lunch with co-workers* who you can laugh with and try new restaurants with. Having fun at lunch is a great way to take your mind off feeling sad.

6. *Leave work early or take a few days off* to rejuvenate yourself until you feel more productive.

By taking some (or all!) of these steps in your personal and professional life, you can better manage depression and its effects on your career, turning negative energy into success. If you think of your career as a house that needs rehabbing, depression is just another element you have to manage. You may not be able to eradicate it completely, but you can lessen its impact on your career and achieve the success you want.

☆ Meet Najeema Davis Washington, Career Depression Overcomer

Najeema Davis Washington is a cross-disciplined, award-winning, senior professional with diverse experience in public affairs and policy, digital marketing, and business and government relations. She studied political science at Spelman College, graduating magna cum laude as a member of the Phi Beta Kappa honor society. She earned a master of public administration (MPA) from the University of North Carolina at Chapel Hill and spent 15 years working in the federal government in Washington, DC, before shifting her career to focus on personal branding, in line with her consulting work on social media and digital strategy.

After several years dealing with career depression, she decided to create a better work-life balance and return to her home in Charleston, South Carolina, to be closer to family and embark upon more rewarding professional experiences. She is now a highly sought-after speaker, panelist, trainer, and presenter who is passionate about social justice.

☆ *What type of workplace or career-related stress, anxiety, or depression have you experienced?*

Najeema Davis Washington, continued

A☆ I experienced stress and career depression with an employer with whom I was not a good fit. Within the first two years of employment, it became clear that my most valuable skills were not being appreciated with this organization. That led to disappointment and denial, and ultimately depression. I experienced stress trying to fit into an environment where I was discouraged and criticized for having aspirations that fit outside the organization. I had never experienced that before—being punished for being ambitious. It was disheartening. It's like the employer ignored the best parts of me and I was merely a cog in the wheel. I often referred to it as being a square peg in a round hole.

There were pockets of positive experiences that, from time to time, led me to believe that I was in a space where my career could develop and thrive. I even began a slight and slow career progression with a promotion and appointment to a coveted detail. But ultimately, I was in denial that I needed to move on. After one particular disappointment, when an opportunity to get off the hamster wheel fell through, my career contentment turned to depression. I began to doubt my skills and felt disappointed in myself for staying in an unsupportive work environment for so long. My unhappiness and disappointment began to bleed over into the everyday work environment; people could tell I was unhappy. Yet, I recognize that a business is a business, and the government is not truly concerned with how happy their employees are. (Although it only makes sense that happier employees perform better.) You can and will be replaced by someone else who wants to fit into that particular machine. My dissatisfaction got to a point where I wanted to take action and find an employer that valued me more.

Q☆ *Why do you think it's so hard for people to cope with or snap out of career depression?*

A☆ People may find it difficult to snap out of career depression because work and work identity are such a part of our lives. In our culture, we are brought up to assign personal value based on our career choices. Professional careers such as doctor, lawyer, engineer, government worker, principal, stockbroker are valued because they can bring financial windfalls and stability or community respect. Employees spend approximately one-third of their lives in the workplace. Feeling valued at work impacts your feelings of well-being and esteem everywhere else. Disappointment

Najeema Davis Washington, continued

at work can easily turn into stress outside of work. Making sure that you derive your personal value outside of your employment can greatly improve feelings of self-worth.

In addition, depression in one's personal life can be a common factor in not snapping out of career depression. In my case, I was adjusting to life with a new diagnosis of bipolar disorder, which I received shortly before accepting my position. A few years later, I experienced tremendous stress after my husband suffered a stroke and died unexpectedly a year and a half later. Nothing in my life's plan prepared me for that. I fell into states of depression several times over the years. I maintained my position with the organization, but my personal unhappiness often spilled over at my workplace. That unhappiness manifested itself as distraction, procrastination, and poor performance. As a person who had excelled in my academic career, it was difficult to accept that I was being assessed as anything less than exceptional in my work environment. My professional assessments were telling me that I was not good enough, which affected my self-esteem and further increased my depression.

Breaking this cycle can be difficult, but one must be intentional to do it. In my case, I sought the support of mental health professionals and committed myself to better personal habits, such as regular exercise. I also utilized my talents outside of the workplace, contributing to professional and civic organizations and conducting freelance work to small businesses and growing brands. Consistently being valued outside of the workplace helped me to become crystal-clear on my worth.

What are some things professionals should attempt to do when they are dealing with stress, anxiety, and depression?

When experiencing career stress, anxiety, or depression, professionals should carefully evaluate and identify the source of the depression. It is important to determine the source in order to address the causes of the depression: Is it the type of work, a particular co-worker, or a supervisor that contributes to the dissatisfaction?

Often depression originating from work can initiate depression at home, and vice versa. Be cognizant of how work depression is impacting your home life. Do your best to leave work at work and be present at home. Conduct breathing exercises before you

Najeema Davis Washington, continued

walk into the house to alleviate work stress. Make a commitment to avoid checking work emails for a few hours after you get home. When you're at home, recharge yourself with the people or the home activities that make you comfortable and less stressed.

Consider regular treatment from a mental health professional. These trained professionals have the skills to help you cope with stress, anxiety, or depression. It's healthy to step outside of your own thinking and allow a professional to give you insights on your issues.

Seek out and consult mentors to discuss professional issues. Your mentors may be familiar with your industry, work environment, supervisors, or co-workers. It's a way to get insights from someone who may have overcome the challenges you are currently facing.

Secure the services of a career coach. A coach can give you tactics or strategies to address the situation that is causing dissatisfaction or conflict in the workplace. A coach can help you gain clarity on your skills and what type of work may be better suited for you.

Determine which personal behaviors need to be changed and commit to changing them, whether it's improving or establishing a better work-life balance, gaining more exercise, or accepting responsibility for when you fell short and performing better going forward.

Depression is often accompanied by feelings of hopelessness. In a professional or work context, that can lead you to believe you are stuck. As a remedy, set goals to get unstuck. That may mean finding a course to improve your skills or taking on projects that may enhance your resume.

☆ *Do you think finding a job you are passionate about decreases your chance of workplace-related stress, anxiety, or depression?*

☆ I think finding a job that you are passionate about helps to decrease those chances; however, it might not take into account personal stress and difficult personalities on the job. Even the "perfect" job can introduce some stress and anxiety. But

Najeema Davis Washington, continued

remembering to gain your worth from the confidence of who you are, what you are capable of, and what you have accomplished will help to decrease those chances of stress, anxiety, or depression.

In my case, after a long period of career depression, I decided to find a new position that valued my greatest skills, and one where I was able to use those on a more frequent basis. My new position is not without some challenges (again, no position is perfect), but I am better equipped to deal with workplace-related stress. I have more confidence in my abilities because I know that they are valued, and I am well-prepared to continue to build a rewarding career.

☆ Meet Karen Millsap,
Resilience and Mindset Coach

Karen Millsap spent a decade in human resources and talent acquisition, where she led numerous training programs, new process rollouts, and change initiatives. At a young age, she suddenly became a widow when her husband was murdered, which completely changed the trajectory of her life. After experiencing a domino effect of other losses, she became acutely aware of the overall lack of support in our society for grieving people. We're all connected through our struggles, from the death of loved ones to life-altering illnesses, divorce, and even job loss. This realization ignited her desire to turn my pain into purpose and pay it forward to help others.

☆ *Tell us a little about your work and how you help your clients manage and overcome personal challenges at work and beyond.*

☆ Egency is a training firm that has designed leadership and culture-training workshops to help organizations create a human-centric culture with compassion and empathy. We've developed and delivered workshops to teach simple, effective ways to create a "people first" culture. Not only does research prove that when you take care of your people, your people will take care of your business, but most importantly, it's the right thing to do.

Karen Millsap, continued

In working with clients one-on-one, I've created the HEAL Method as a framework to help the brokenhearted heal with clarity. This is the pathway back to a whole heart through building healthy habits, practicing emotional regulation, and focusing on self-care.

H stands for *healthy boundaries*. It's important to set healthy boundaries while we are healing and focused on personal growth. We can't allow others to poison what we're trying to grow. There are many ways to set healthy boundaries: emotional, mental, and physical. It applies to the relationships we have with friends and family and even broadens out to our connection to technology and social media. Protecting our minds and our hearts from outside influences and negative energy is critical to experiencing a healthy healing journey.

E stands for *embrace emotions*. There's no healing if there's no feeling. It's important to learn how to identify our emotions and then properly manage them. Otherwise, we'll resist the flow of life. There will always be ups and downs, so if we don't learn how to control our erratic feelings, then our feelings will control us.

A stands for *accept what is*. We can't change what's happened in the past, and we can't control what's going to happen in the future. This is why accepting where we are right now is absolutely critical in the healing process. We may not like it, but if we first accept where we are, then we can start moving forward in the right direction with intention.

And **L** stands for *love yourself*. This is where self-care comes into play. The truth is, we often don't know how to love ourselves properly. There are simple habits that you can start doing today that will radically transform your quality of life. Loving yourself means loving your *whole self*—your physical, mental, emotional, and spiritual well-being.

⭐ *How do you see stress, anxiety, and depression affecting people at work?*

⭐ If we feel anxious or stressed about work, or if life throws a curveball, some of the first emotions we all feel are isolation, detachment, grief, and loneliness. We've been programmed to not speak up when things at work become overwhelming and to "leave your personal stuff at the door," which is impossible. Even if we do our best to

Karen Millsap, continued

suppress emotions and try to put on a "front" while in the office, we're still carrying the weight of these feelings wherever we go.

Whether you've just experienced a personal tragedy or you're amidst a crisis that's causing emotional distress, you're more than likely experiencing an internal battle between processing the tough emotions and trying to ignore them.

Let me tell you, this is normal! You are not alone.

⭐ *How can people manage these elements of their work lives?*

⭐ Grief, stress, and anxiety produce physical and psychological side effects that must be worked through, not suppressed. When life gets messy, it can pour over into our presence, our behavior, and our performance at work. You can alleviate some of the struggle by following these tips.

First, be intentional and mindful of the energy that you are putting into your body. What are you feeding your body? Most people don't realize the overlap of our physical, emotional, and mental well being. There are foods that can help combat things like stress and depression (a wonderful book that gives a super-easy breakdown of what foods are best for our mental well-being is *The Brain Fog Fix* by Dr. Mike Dow).

For example, if you know you have a busy day ahead, and you're already overwhelmed by complex emotions, eat power meals with lots of nutrients and energy. Keep in mind what you eat will help the way you show up at work! If you eat like trash, you will feel like trash.

You'll be surprised how much your mood, mental clarity, and productivity will improve with intentional food choices. Start your day with a good breakfast so you're fueled with nutrients and wholesome goodness. Intentionally pack or order healthy lunches to get the proper energy to keep you going through the day. Veggies should definitely be included! And if you can, eat lunch outside. Vitamin D is a great mood booster, and exposure to the sun helps our bodies produce more vitamin D. Lastly, we all love to snack throughout the day. But don't eat junk food—it will only make you feel worse. Enjoy protein bars, fruits and nuts, turkey jerky, or even dark chocolate if you have a sweet tooth.

Karen Millsap, continued

Second, practice a technique I call the Rule of Three. We may not like to admit it, but it's very common to feel stressed and overwhelmed by our never-ending to-do list. However, the reality is we can only do ONE thing at a time. The Rule of Three helps you focus on a manageable workload by identifying only the most important things that should be at the top of your priority list.

Here's how I do it. At the end of each day, I think about what tasks need to be completed the following day, and I write them on my whiteboard. You can use sticky notes if you'd like. This gets my days started with a clear direction. After completing each task, I cross it from the whiteboard, and the sense of accomplishment makes me smile each time. Oh, and don't start a new list of three until you've completed the first set!

Not only will this technique help you to stay on track with your priorities, but it's also a confidence booster because it helps you see your progress throughout the day.

When my husband died, I was initially shocked, and then immediately slipped into a fog. When I look back, I think I remained in that fog for nearly two years. Everyone around me kept saying that I was "strong," when truthfully, I was just operating on autopilot. The best thing I could've done when I returned to work was be vulnerable, open, and honest with my boss about where I was mentally and emotionally.

4

THE REHAB YOU CAREER BLUEPRINT

You cannot rehab your career without first creating a blueprint. Your career blueprint is the design phase of the Rehab YOU framework. When you build a house for new construction or rehab an existing house, you create a blueprint before the actual work begins. Most blueprints are created by designers and architects. Since you will be the designer and architect of your own career, it's time to sketch out how you want it to look. Most home buyers refer to these blueprints as house plans or floor plans;

they include room design and layout, wiring plans, and even notes on materials. Your career blueprint will similarly have multiple elements, all intended to bring together a cohesive plan for your new, rehabbed career.

The key components of your career floor plan should include:

→ *Career path.* What industry do you want to work in or continue to work in?

→ *Career location.* What cities, states, or countries do you desire to work in?

→ *Career salary.* What is your immediate salary goal? What are your long-term salary goals?

→ *Career dimensions.* How far do you want to go in your career? Describe your career growth over the next five years.

→ *Career spaces and rooms.* Where do you want to work? Do you prefer small, medium, or larger organizations?

→ *Career appliances.* What extra incentives could an organization offer you that would make you happy? Training, work from home, benefits, vacation time, etc.

→ *Career builders.* Who do you need in your life to assist you as you build your career? Identify mentors, instructors, recruiters, colleagues, or managers who can help you build the career you deserve.

In this chapter, you will read about each of these components of your career blueprint and focus in on what elements are most important to you during your rehab process.

Career Path

Look at your career path as if you were picking out a new apartment, condo, or house to live in. No matter where you are in your life, you have to decide on a design for your existing or new career path. You may be building a "starter home" in the form of an entry-level job, or maybe you are advancing in your career and want to build a bigger "house" (expand into a more challenging field). Maybe you are a retiree who is planning to downsize into a "condo" because you want to work less as you transition into retirement.

Think about where you are in life and where you want to go. Here are some questions you should ask yourself:

→ Am I happy in my current industry?
→ Do I want to make a lateral move into a different segment in my current industry?
→ Do I want to switch gears and do something entirely different?
→ Do I want to add value with a new or updated skill set?
→ Do I want to dial back my responsibilities?

Designing your career path can be a fun and exciting process for college graduates, professionals, and retirees. The great thing about your career path is that it can be designed and redesigned multiple times. Some career paths will be designed correctly the first time, and some will have to be redesigned as you go through career changes. Career changes are awesome (even the ones that might come as a surprise), so don't feel bad if you have to redesign your career path many times. You will never stop leveling up your career path as you Rehab YOU.

Career Location

When a potential owner is purchasing a home, location is one of the most important factors. It's the same with your career. Professionals should always research the cities, states, and countries they are considering working in. The location determines how many jobs are available and how much you can make based on the cost of living in that area. Consider whether you would prefer to work in a big city, small city, town, or rural area. Some career paths do better in certain cities. When you do your research and identify a career location that is right for you and your family, it really helps you pinpoint your potential salary, job-market options, and local employers.

For instance, I am in the tech industry by trade, and within the Washington, DC, metropolitan area, there is a surplus of six-figure technology jobs. There are more open tech jobs than available professionals to fill them. It's a good problem to have if you are a job seeker. On average, five to ten recruiters call or email me about new roles each week. However, the abundance of jobs does not outweigh the fact that it's expensive to live in Washington, DC. Conversely, in a smaller city like Columbia, South Carolina, the cost of living is much lower, but there is not a surplus of jobs like there is in Washington, DC. So as I worked to create my own career blueprint, I looked to online resources to help me navigate the pros and cons when deciding where I wanted to live and work. Glassdoor.com helped me identify my career options, company locations, and salary potential in this area.

Career Salary

Think of your career salary as the price of a house after it is built or rehabbed. You have to identify how much you want to get paid today as well as your future worth after you have enhanced your personal brand with more work experience and expertise. You deserve an annual salary based on the finished product you will be after you rehab your personal brand. As you create your career blueprint, identify your high, medium, and low salary ranges—and remember, all these numbers are relative to your location. For example, homes in South Carolina cost much less than homes in Washington, DC. It's the same with professionals' salaries. I can earn $20,000 to $30,000 more per year as a tech industry project manager in Washington, DC than I could in South Carolina, but my expenses are higher here as well.

What are your career salary goals? Identify a salary range you would like to make now. In 2019, I started a new role as a senior project manager at a federal agency managing digital IT projects. Before I took the role, I identified my career worth on Glassdoor. Senior project manager roles in the Washington, DC area pay between $77,000 and $149,000 per year, so that was my window to shoot for.

If your career area has a similarly wide range of salaries, it can be hard to know what to ask for. As you Rehab YOU, you don't want to lowball yourself. The key is to know your worth and identify a realistic salary that aligns with your current career level. You may not start off making six figures (my first job out of college was with Verizon, making $55,000 per year), but you will climb the pay scale as you move forward. As I gained more experience, education, and expertise, I worked my way up to the mid-six figures. Your career salary will continue to evolve along with your personal brand.

Career Dimensions

When you create a blueprint for a house, you have to consider the dimensions of the home: the total square footage, the sizes of the rooms, etc. As a professional, you must identify your career growth dimensions and think about how far you plan to go in your career path. Some professionals aim to be a director or manager at a company, while others would like to be an analyst or an executive assistant in a specific field. Your career dimensions are key measurements of your career floor plan. How big do you want your personal brand to become? Not everyone wants to rise to the top of a company, and that's OK. When you are rehabbing you, it's all about setting your own career expectations. Success is not defined by how big your title is or how much money you make. Career rehab is about defining the career dimensions that will make you happy.

How do you set your career dimensions? Try these three steps:

1. Identify what type of role you would like now.
2. Identify whether you want a promotion in the next three to five years and what type of role you would want to have as you gain more experience.
3. Make a list of any education, certifications, and training you may need to take on more advanced roles and responsibility.

As you set your career dimensions, aim high because it helps you increase your career salary. As your dimensions become larger, you have a better chance of selling your personal brand to companies that will value your qualities and skill set.

Career Spaces and Rooms

Before most people purchase a home, they identify what types of rooms and spaces they are looking for: Do they need a large kitchen? A home office? A family room? It's the same for your career: You have to identify what types of career spaces and rooms you want to grow in. These spaces and rooms represent the types of organizations, companies, and cultures that will work well for your career path. They should include attributes and atmospheres that you can thrive in on a daily basis. Some of the "cool geeks" (recent college graduates) I work with don't always know what types of rooms and spaces will work well for their personalities. But I do have some corporate rebels who love working in innovative and collaborative offices. Traditional office spaces don't make them productive or happy about coming to work. Then I have some career dropouts who have worked 30 years in a traditional cubicle environment and truly enjoyed their careers. But they may not have had anything to compare it to because they stayed in the same job their entire career. Perhaps they would have enjoyed an open space even more.

Your work environment is your second home if you are working ten-hour days, meaning you are at work 42 percent of the time Monday through Friday. If you want your career to thrive, you have to work in spaces and rooms that promote productivity and engagement with your co-workers and leadership teams. So it's key to identify companies that have the right rooms and spaces, both literally and figuratively. You can research companies' cultures by exploring their websites and reading employee reviews on Glassdoor. Some companies will offer tours when you interview. When I interviewed with Deloitte LLP for a position as a senior consultant, they gave us a tour of their innovative labs, conference rooms, and cafeteria. It was a great way to sell the company culture to me before I accepted their job offer.

To determine what kinds of career spaces and rooms you want, consider the following issues:

→ Identify whether you would thrive best in a small, medium, or large organization.

→ Ask yourself what type of office space you like: traditional, open office, a co-working space, or working from home.

→ Would you like to work alone in a cubicle or office?

→ Would you like to work on a team that collaborates often using web-conferencing technologies, smart TVs, or white-boards?

As you work at several jobs, you will become more familiar with what spaces work well for you. Keeping employee happiness in mind, many companies now design workspaces and environments that can increase overall productivity. And happiness matters: According to a 2015 experiment at the University of Warwick with more than 700 participants, increasing people's happiness also increases their productivity by 12 percent.

Career Appliances

The most attractive assets of a home are usually its appliances, electronics, and furniture. These three components drive how a person will feel when they live in the home. Appliances, electronics, and furniture are similar to a company's perks and incentives. I like to call these incentives the "career appliances." Career appliances drive the happiness and joy employees feel about their jobs. We all want perks, work-life balance, extra time off, etc.

Some of the best career appliance incentives increase employee happiness and productivity. For example, some companies allow their employees to bring their dogs to work and provide personal sabbaticals and free lunches. Other popular perks include gym memberships, flexible work hours, work-from-home options, wellness programs, on-site stores and health services, continuing education programs, tuition reimbursement, and even trips to exotic locales. All these perks are great, but which ones really speak to you?

What do you need to feel appreciated by an employer? How do you identify the career appliances you need to be happy? Start by taking stock of the following:

→ Identify company incentives that align with your personal goals.
→ Identify company incentives that will help you reach your career goals.
→ Identify work-life balance perks that will keep your stress, anxiety, and depression under control.
→ Focus on perks, benefits, and incentives that can benefit your family.

Career Builders

As you create your career floor plan, you will need a team of builders. Most successful professionals call on mentors, managers, colleagues, and recruiters to help them land new career roles and promotions. As you design your career blueprint, create an all-star team of recruiters who will help you get the salary you deserve. Then work with hiring managers to learn more about your career appliances.

When home buyers purchase an existing home, they use a real estate agent to help them find one that's a good fit. When they are looking to build a brand-new home, they have to hire the right builders to construct it for them. As you create the blueprint or floor plan for your career, you have to identify both. *Career builders* help you build your career, while *career agents* help you find the right job for your career. Career builders are mentors, career coaches, and industry leaders. Career agents are headhunters, recruiters, and HR professionals.

Career builders provide industry-specific expertise to help you succeed in your career. Career agents bring new opportunities to you that may be a good fit. Career builders can sometimes help you obtain your dream job through their professional network as well. But they usually offer professional and moral support when your job isn't going well. Career agents help you find a new job when things go wrong. Your career agent should always be a resource to help you find a new job with the right salary, benefits, and commute.

Over the past five years, I have created a network on LinkedIn of more than 5,000 career agents and builders. At any time, I can reach out to them to help me or my clients land a job at companies like Microsoft, Booz Allen Hamilton, Intel, Google, Facebook, and various federal government agencies.

☆ Meet Jeff Gothelf, UX Designer and Author

Jeff Gothelf is a UX designer who, with the help of many other smart people, helped solve the challenge of making user experience design work with the agile development process. He co-wrote a book called *Lean UX* that started a global conversation on redefining design in software. Along with co-author Josh Seiden, he wrote a business book called *Sense & Respond* to help executives rethink how they manage their companies in the face of the AI revolution. These days, he works as a coach, consultant, and keynote speaker for midsize and large organizations, helping them drive their digital transformation and increase their agility to bring them closer to their customers.

☆ *What is the best approach for professionals to try to create prototypes for their career blueprint? How can professionals career brainstorm—wireframing, sketching, etc.?*

☆ Job change can be risky. Jumping to another role, position, or company can be a great move or it can end up being a ditch you find yourself stuck in. To de-risk these moves, I've often used "moonlighting" as a strategy to find the next opportunity. Moonlighting is where you work a side job while maintaining your full-time job. It's part time and happens after hours. It allows you to try a new type of work, client, or employer without the risk of losing your day job. If the feedback from that experience is positive, you've successfully de-risked the move and can make a more evidence-based decision about the change.

Another way I've sketched out my career plan is writing about it. I've written articles about jobs that I would like to have. Sometimes these jobs existed and other times they didn't. My goal was to get the idea out there and, if possible, lead the conversation about those jobs. If the right people engage in that writing, it can lead

Jeff Gothelf, continued

to new opportunities more in line with where you'd like to go next, and the best part is that you literally wrote your own ticket. Your description becomes the job.

How can professionals incorporate continuous discovery as they build their career like a product?

This is a deliberate effort where you are constantly thinking about where you'd like your career to go. The best approach I've seen here is to continuously engage with the community you work in. Tweet, blog, write, post photos, attend events, and put your ideas out there. See how the community reacts. Find the tribe of people who support your career vision and build relationships with them. This is a constant process of build, measure, and learn. You float an idea, see how the community reacts, and then build on the learning from that feedback. Ultimately, the people in your community will associate you with those ideas, and when opportunities arise in those fields, you'll be the first person they call.

As a professional creates their career blueprint, there may be challenges and career ups and downs. How can professionals feel OK with giving themselves permission to fail?

The easy answer here is to build a financial safety net. Save enough money so that if you make a bad decision, the financial impact is reduced due to these savings. However, I know this is not an option for many people. In these cases, I'll just share my experience. I've been terrified my whole career of getting fired or choosing a bad employer or job: *What would happen? Could I quit? Would I find another job? How long will it take? Can I feed my kids?*

What I've learned time and time again, each time I've failed, is that nothing gives you more of a kick in the ass and spurs positive change than these "failures." They are situations that force you to make quick decisions, tighten up your public persona and presence, reach out to colleagues and leaders, and inspire you to try things you normally wouldn't try. The best opportunities I've had have come when something I did deliberately failed. The community and the effort I'd put in up to that point kick in to provide new paths to explore, and quickly. It may sound contrived, but each of these "failures" is a learning opportunity and a period of time that forces you to rethink your path—which is never a bad thing.

5

BE A BRAND, NOT AN EMPLOYEE

Congratulations! You have conquered how to DESIGN your career blueprint. Now it's time to BUILD your personal brand as you Rehab YOU. Building your personal brand is all about making that career blueprint feel and look good. It's like adding new furniture and decorations to your home; it feels good to walk into a home that has been lovingly decorated by its owner. When you go into those career rooms and new professional spaces, you will have a solid personal brand that looks and feels good, too.

Sometimes to get the salary you desire or get promoted to a higher level, you have to enhance your personal brand. Most of the time, when we think of the word *brand,* companies like Nike, Amazon, and Apple come to mind. But those are company brands, and you are a personal brand. Remember, we are rehabbing you, not the company you work for. They already have a brand.

So do you view yourself as an employee or a brand? In this chapter, you will learn how to see your education, experience, and expertise as a brand. You will also learn how to let go of the employee mindset by valuing your professional relationships and stop undervaluing your work tasks. Finally, you will learn how to embrace a branding mindset by keeping track of your professional performance metrics and delivering quality work products and communication. This mindset shift will help you build a solid personal brand and make you highly marketable, both within your current organization and as you attempt to seek new opportunities.

Identify Your Brand

Now it's time to change how you view yourself at work. Most of us had or still have an employee mindset. When you are an employee, you often think you are expected to only do what you are told, and you don't always see your knowledge as valuable. The employee mindset does not challenge leadership or other team members to enhance or create a new, innovative way to perform an existing process.

We all know people who do just enough to keep their jobs and don't really have a vision for their careers. Some employees may not feel empowered to do great work or just don't like their jobs. So having a personal brand mindset is the last thing on their minds. But their institutional knowledge or in-depth understanding of a process makes them a subject-matter expert, even if they don't realize it. The great news is that *all* of us are brands—we just don't always know how to leverage our education, experience, and expertise to grow and scale them.

When you have a branding mindset, you think of your expertise and knowledge like a product or service. Brands offer unique products or experiences that you can't get anywhere else. It's the same in the professional world: You have to go to work and provide expertise and unique experiences with your team members or clients that no one else offers. This personal branding can be experienced in the way you deliver your task, how you dress, or how you conduct yourself in meetings. People with a brand mindset present their best selves every day and constantly work to enhance their knowledge. We all know a popular team member, high-profile leader, or elected official within our organizations whom people love and respect. They have developed a solid personal brand where they offer a specialty expertise or have accomplished amazing goals throughout their career.

People often mistakenly believe that you have to work in a high-visibility role to have a brand. Whether you work as a secretary, trash collector, or computer engineer, you have a personal brand. If you want to level up your mindset from an employee to a brand, you have to change the way you think about what you have to offer.

YOU are the expert in your field—so act like it! Stop undervaluing your education, experience, and expertise—they are your core edifiers. You are a BRAND, and you must learn how to edify yourself by identifying your brand. To do that, you can use the Three Es:

1. *Education.* High school diploma, college degree, or professional certification
2. *Experience.* Volunteer, internship, or work experience
3. *Expertise.* Focused areas of knowledge, methodologies, tools, and technologies

Allow your edifiers to build the foundation of your personal brand. This foundation will help you get noticed by career builders and career agents who are looking to staff new employees.

Then you can use these three ways to maximize your identifiers:

1. *Education.* Always include your earned diplomas, college degrees, and professional certifications on your resume, LinkedIn profile, and job board profiles.
2. *Experience.* List and describe your volunteer and work experience on your resume going back 15 years.

3. *Expertise.* Be descriptive and tell how you were able to apply your education with your experience on a daily basis as you completed complex projects.

By using the Three Es and the three ways you maximize them, you've already started cultivating your personal brand. The next step is to change how YOU think about your career.

Let Go of the Employee Mindset

You can begin to let go of the employee mindset when you see value in all the different ways you work and communicate at work. Whenever you communicate—via email, in person, and on the phone—you are displaying your personal brand. Writing an email or answering a question in a meeting is a key opportunity for people to recognize your expertise and personality. When you rise above mediocrity every day, people will become a fan of your work ethic and will start to love you as a person, too. Employees find a way to only do what's asked of them, but personal brands find a way to market themselves through their unique offerings and experiences.

Here are four ways to begin to let go of your employee mindset:

1. Stop undervaluing the tasks you do every day.
2. Value your relationships with internal stakeholders, external stakeholders, and clients you meet with regularly.
3. Start finding new ways to speak at staff meetings via presentations, briefings, and conference calls.
4. Go out of your way to attend all-hands meetings and workplace parties.

Embrace a Branding Mindset

As you let go of your employee mindset, you will begin to adopt a branding mindset. Remember, you have designed your career blueprint, so now it's time to create a personal brand that matches your career goals, desires, and dreams. When you create your personal brand, there are no true boundaries. You are free to build it as you wish.

Here are three ways to embrace a branding mindset:

1. Big or small, everything you do at work is an asset; always deliver quality products, customer service, and information.
2. Display great communication skills in meetings, conference calls, phone calls, and emails with everyone you come in contact with.
3. Write down your weekly accomplishments and keep track of your performance metrics.

You add value in everything you do and everyone you come in contact with, even if it doesn't always feel like it. The best way to present your personal brand is to always strive to go above and beyond.

Build You, Being You

As you build your personal brand as a cool geek, corporate rebel, or career dropout, authenticity is a great asset. When you align with organizations that embrace your personality and expertise as a college graduate, professional, or retiree, it creates a smooth transition if leadership and colleagues feel comfortable with you displaying your personal brand at all times. Not every company will like your authentic self, so it's important to assess the work environment and see how much it can handle of you simply being you. This is not to say that you should have no filter on what you say or wear your pajamas to work. What it does mean is that you can bring your authentic self to work by taking part in personal enrichment activities that help build your brand and use those experiences as touchpoints in your daily work, whether in meetings or in personal conversations with colleagues. To that end, here are ten ways to build on your education, experience, and expertise for your personal brand:

1. Work on challenging work-related projects.
2. Enroll in training related to your job or career goals.
3. Earn more professional certifications.
4. Read one industry-related book per month.

5. Read one career-related blog or article per day.
6. Watch one or two short industry-related videos on YouTube or Udemy per week.
7. Listen to industry-related podcasts.
8. Volunteer to work on cross-collaboration projects and detail opportunities.
9. Attend free professional conferences, virtual webinars, and workshops throughout the year.
10. Connect with experts within your organization and pick their brains for new knowledge.

If you want a solid personal brand, you must go beyond the basics of getting a degree, a new job, or a certification and help your brand grow beyond the confines of your current cubicle. The best corporate brands keep advancing their products and services by offering new products, marketing those products in new ways, and collaborating with media outlets and companies to advance their brands. You have to do the same thing if you want to increase your compensation and succeed against your competition.

Adopt Celebrity Branding

Celebrities are the royalty of personal branding. Athletes, actors, and musicians use their personal brands to market their sports, movies, and songs. It's the same with your personal brand: You have to mash up who you are as a person with what you do. Consider Beyoncé. Consumers love to buy and listen to her songs because she includes her personal life in her music. We have watched her brand evolve, first as a member of Destiny's Child, then as a solo artist, and now as a mother and wife. She has bridged the gap between being a musical icon with her personal identity as an African-American woman from Texas. No one does personal branding better.

As a professional, you have to go beyond feeling like you are just an employee and bring some of yourself into your work (just like Beyoncé does). Personal branding helps you create an emotional connection with your manager, co-workers, and stakeholders in all your staff meetings, phone calls, and emails. You can become an office celebrity: the rock-star professional who always delivers quality work or dazzles the company at briefings. The office is your stage; it's your time to shine the same way athletes shine on the football field or basketball court.

But you have to keep evolving in your knowledge. The same way athletes work at off-season training, you have to train up your personal brand by taking classes online and reading books. Enhance your personal brand, focusing on what you need to please your customers, clients, or management team. You are a champion, and to win at work you have to develop your personal brand for your professional playoffs. The professional playoffs are when you learn the most on the job, the challenging times that prepare you for the championship game. These playoffs may come when your project hits a difficult sticking point or when you have to learn how to execute a new play (new technology) so your team can win. But you were built to win, and as you Rehab YOU, it will become increasingly easy to develop your personal brand like a celebrity does. Always see the star in you and remember that you have something special to offer the world. Keep defining and branding it.

Small Things Build Your Brand

We all take for granted the small things we do each day and forget to add these tasks to our resume. But it's those tiny projects, administrative tasks, and everyday communications that help build your brand. As you renovate your career, you also have to gut your resume and LinkedIn profile and add those small things. They count! When you start thinking of yourself as a brand, you can make the small things look BIG.

For instance, I created my first real professional resume when I was working on my bachelor's degree in computer technology and interning as an office clerk. I wanted to land a job in my tech field, but all I was doing was clerical work. So one day I took a notepad, brainstormed everything I did as an office clerk, and made it sound more computer-focused. I was becoming a brand, and I didn't even know it.

Below are some examples of how I revised my resume before I graduated from college so I could land a job at Verizon as a network control supervisor. You can easily adapt this technique to fit your own situation:

→ Changed "Emailed stakeholders" to "Utilized Microsoft Outlook to draft and send emails"
→ Changed "Tracked information in spreadsheets" to "Created and optimized data using Microsoft Access"
→ Changed "Drafted letters and memorandums" to "Composed letters and memorandums using Microsoft Word"
→ Changed "Answered telephone calls" to "Utilized electronic telephone systems to answer and transfer calls"

See what I did there? I increased the value of my day-to-day activities with just a few well-chosen words. Your small duties hold a lot of value; it's all in how you present it. Are you presenting yourself as an employee or a brand? Brand-magnify every accomplishment, new role, or new task so you can market it in future job interviews. When you make your small tasks and accomplishments look big, you can sell them for big bucks. The bigger your brand looks, the wider your marketability will be in this competitive job market. Personal brands secure solid careers; employees get average jobs.

☆ Meet Peter Economy,
Branding Expert and Business Author

Peter Economy is a bestselling business author, ghostwriter, developmental editor, and publishing consultant with more than 100 books to his credit (and more than two million copies sold). He has also written more than 1,400 columns as the Leadership Guy, Inc.

☆Q *How does an employee shift their mindset from being an employee to being a brand?*

☆A The workplace has changed fundamentally over the past several decades. Before, people had jobs for life, and they pretty much stayed with just one or two companies for their entire careers. They didn't need to worry much about marketing themselves or being a brand. Today, people change jobs and companies all the time. This makes it absolutely essential for people to develop a personal-brand mindset to stand out from the rest of the pack. You *are* your brand. In the words of Susan Vitale, CMO at iCIMS, a provider of HR software, "Having a killer personal brand is no longer an option, but a requirement when it comes to landing that job you've always wanted." The mindset shift comes from understanding that it's not enough to just be an employee, no matter how good you might be. You've got to establish your brand, too. It's what your current and future employers will know you by.

☆Q *What do the initial stages of brand development look like for an employee?*

☆A First, brainstorm your brand. Who are you? What is your purpose in life? What value do you provide to your boss? Your co-workers? Your customers? Your community? The world? What are the qualities and characteristics of the brand that is you? Second, promote your brand. Some may call it bragging, but the savvy job hunter knows that singing your own praises works to improve and support your personal brand. Complete a big project at work? Post about it. Head up a successful volunteer activity in your community? Post about it. Cook a nice meal for two? Don't post about it. Nothing bothers the masses more than social media oversharers, especially when your targeted audience is your future boss. Don't forget, your personal brand is a supplement to your resume. Show potential employers you are active in your industry and successful in your endeavors with regular—not obsessive—Twitter posts or LinkedIn updates. Third, make sure you do good work and that you constantly provide

Peter Economy, continued

more value and not less. When you do, your brand will be even stronger and people will seek you out.

⭐ *What are the best ways employees can create their digital footprint for their personal brand?*

⭐ If it's online, everyone can see it—including current and potential employers. Approximately 76 percent of recruiters say that they always or sometimes perform a Google search on candidates before hiring them, and 40 percent report finding online information that has disqualified a candidate from consideration. Review all of your social-media profiles and make sure every aspect is complete and what you want prospective employers to know about you. From favorite books to past work experience—it all counts. Remember: This is no time to be shy. Be positive, be honest, be accurate, and be you.

BUILD YOUR BRAND BY "DATING" JOBS

Now that you have started to think about developing your personal brand for your career, it's time to build your brand by "dating" jobs. You can't expand your career dimensions and be present in different career spaces and rooms without trying out various jobs to see how well they suit you. When you date jobs, you can rapidly and easily increase your career salary because you are constantly landing new jobs and learning skills as you travel your career path.

Your brand is the most important element of your career, but you must always build upon it by thinking, *How can this bigger brand [the company] help me reach my goals as I build my personal brand?* Look at it like this: At the core of working at a job is a relationship between you and the company. We spend more time at work than we do with our families, so it's a big commitment! That's why I love the idea of dating your jobs, because they are short-term to long-term relationships with your manager, your co-workers, and the work you do every day. When you date people, you're spending time with someone you like, but you're not committing to them for the long term. It's the same with a job. You can find value in going to a job you like, with a good salary, team members, culture fit, benefits, and work, without getting "married" to it.

In this chapter, you will learn how to date (and speed date!) jobs, get the most out of your role, and then strategically move on. For instance, you will learn how working on challenging projects can give you unique exposure and enhance your professional experience for the next job. Dating jobs is a career-rehab concept that helps you not feel "stuck" in a job while continuing to leverage your personal brand.

What Does It Mean to Date Jobs?

Dating jobs gives you direct access to experience and exposure that can only benefit you as you build your personal brand. In your career, you have to date jobs to figure out what type of organization, culture, job duties, and leadership styles work best for your goals. When you date new people, you get new experiences and exposure to new personalities and backgrounds. Companies likewise have personalities (called "company cultures"), and their background represents how long the company has been established or what their specialized services or products include. Have you ever been on a date where you learned more about the other person's life and background, or gone to a new place for dinner? These dating concepts are called *unique experiences* and *unique exposure*—and the same concepts apply when you date a job to build your brand. Here's the formula (followed by a quick explanation of each element that helps you build your brand):

Unique Experiences + Unique Exposure = Building Your Brand

→ *Unique Experiences.* When you date a job, you learn new skills and tools. The more complex projects you work on, the more you gain valuable experience that will help you move on to the next job.

→ *Unique Exposure.* Those unique experiences give you increasing opportunities to work on complex projects and meet new people on external-facing projects. This exposure helps build your brand as you move from job to job until you find one you want to marry (stay in for the long haul). Unique exposure is a great way to build, market, and sell your personal brand.

Put these two elements together, and you have a new layer to add to your personal career brand.

Speed Dating Jobs

Speed dating jobs is about taking new career opportunities that can help you enhance your existing skills, learn a new cutting-edge skill set, and work in a new role that will help you earn more money—then move on. The more you learn, the more you should earn. You may not be sure what type of company is a good fit for you, so speed dating jobs gives you the opportunity to benefit from new project challenges, training, and new certifications. Speed dating is for career hustlers who are ready to sell themselves. If you are not satisfied with the current job you are dating, it's time to move on to the next job.

At one of my lowest career moments, I began to find happiness once I left a good federal government job after more than five years of being miserable. I took a job with Deloitte Consulting for less than a year, then I joined a small consulting firm named Sevatec for a year, and then I worked for a third company called American Systems remotely for 18 months. Each time I learned new technologies. While I was at Deloitte, I became a Certified ScrumMaster® (CSM®) and learned more about the Adobe Experience Manager content-management system. My knowledge there transferred to Sevatec, where I led a technical team overseeing web development and design for embassy websites across the world. This project taught me more about cloud computing and automating deployments. I then took some time off to think about what type of job I wanted next and decided I wanted to work remotely so I could build my career coaching practice. I next landed a six-figure job through a recruiter, working on a website user experience improvement project for the Department of Defense. I was learning fast, and I was speed dating in the private sector, enjoying the unique experiences and exposure.

It was an exciting time for me professionally, but not everyone wants to take the leap into speed dating jobs. As a career coach, I have observed that most professionals are scared of the idea of dating jobs. They are accustomed to job security, and leaving their job of 15 years is a frightening thought. They wonder whether staying in a job for only a short time will reflect poorly on their resume (it won't) or whether they can handle jumping from company to company quickly (they can).

Taking a big step like speed dating jobs starts with wanting career happiness more than you want your current job. Being open to dating jobs requires you to be open to new roles and new companies. It also requires you to learn how to detach from jobs. Brands are detachable when business partnerships don't work out. I want you to learn how to keep going despite bad work experiences or staying too long in a job that may have been a good experience at one time but has since run its course. Basically, you have to be less emotional; focus most of your energy on how you will win while you are dating jobs. And sometimes, you can only win by walking away.

Dating Jobs Duration Model

Dating jobs looks different depending on where you are in your career journey. As you build your career blueprint, you may date jobs quickly or slowly. I have identified the length of time you should date a job, depending on your career goals. If you find career happiness, you may not date jobs as frequently as someone who is still looking for career love—and that's OK. Choose a timeline that works for you.

Speed Job Dating for Cool Geeks

As a college graduate, you should date your first professional role for at least two to three years. With less than five years of experience, you may need 24 months to learn new skills, attend professional training, and start building your professional network at one organization. Cool geeks don't always start out speed dating jobs as fast as corporate rebels and career dropouts. You may already have some idea of your career plans, but you have to see how your first two years of working professionally turn out.

Speed Job Dating for Corporate Rebels

As a midlevel or senior-level professional, you should date jobs for one to two years, because at this point in your career, you should have more than five years of professional experience and some idea of what you want: the role, salary, and culture fit. You may be fed up at this point in your career, so you should be ready to speed date jobs until you find the right fit.

Speed Job Dating for Career Dropouts

As a senior-level employee or retiree, you may be ready to start a business full time or ready to start a new career after retirement. You may need to date your current role and cheat on it with your business idea or new career interests while you are still working (i.e., work a side hustle). Career dropouts are ready to drop their career for their dream, but you need to prepare for one to three years in advance before you make the break official. While dating your current role, you should be learning the skills of your new career path for retirement. You should also launch your business and brand, market, and sell it to consumers for one to three years before you officially become a career dropout.

By this point, you may be thinking speed dating jobs is a bad idea. But dating jobs helps you build your brand. Your chief loyalty should be to you, developing the professional skills that will help you become more marketable. But while you are gaining this experience and expanding your network, always give your best at work. I want you to give 100 percent of yourself while you are working for a company eight to ten hours a day. At the same time, be sure to identify what's in it for you. After all, Fortune 500 companies are making millions or even billions of dollars off their employees. You have to care about you—because the company certainly won't.

Benefits in Dating Jobs

Whether you are dating jobs slowly or speed dating, you will be able to discover the benefits for your brand in most organizations. If you don't find any, you should dump that job as soon as you find a better one to date. Think of dating jobs as being "friends with benefits." You're not terribly serious about each other, but you have a good time and enjoy some extra perks. While the job is treating you well, you should stay and try to soak up all those benefits, like paid education, professional training, high compensation, and global travel. In other words, what's in it for YOU? How can dating jobs benefit your unique experience and exposure?

These are the five main benefits of dating jobs:

1. *Paid education.* Many organizations help employees pay for their college degrees. When you date a job that will pay for your higher education, you may have to work there a little longer. But you will leave debt free, and you will earn an associate's, bachelor's, master's, or Ph.D. while you are there. Student loan debt is high for most professionals, so I encourage you to take advantage of any free opportunities to further your education.

2. *Professional training.* Each year, most professionals are given a training budget by their organization, which covers the cost of one or more classes. You can find job-related training to help you learn new skills. After you complete the training, you can add those courses to your resume. Professional training increases your marketability and gives you more efficient ways to do your job.

3. *Higher compensation.* The more jobs you date, the more money you will make. Over the years you will gain experience in speed dating, and your brand's value will continue to increase. If you are going to work at your job for eight to ten hours every day, you might as well get paid top dollar for being there.

4. *Network expansion.* When you expand your network, you are increasing your brand's net worth. The more people you know, the more you can grow, so dating jobs is full of opportunities for network expansion. Just like celebrities, the more people you are connected to, the easier it is to collaborate on various projects in your field. Your network expansion is an asset to your brand.

5. *Global travel.* One of the luxuries of working for companies that hire travel consultants or professionals is that you may have to do some traveling for your job. You can see the world, stay in nice hotels, and learn about other cultures on the company's dime, not your own. Global travel is a priceless experience for professionals who may be considering relocation or who just love to travel.

Remember: Building your brand by identifying what education, skills, certifications, training, and professional experience you will need to move forward is made possible by getting exposure to many segments of your industry. Some of my career-coaching clients who landed jobs at Oracle, Microsoft, and Boeing maximized their unique experience and exposure with other benefits that enhanced their personal brand. These clients learned how to date jobs by acquiring unique exposure and experience while working on high-visibility projects supporting global missions and creating innovative products and services for the Departments of State, the Navy, and Defense. By dating jobs, they have leveraged their personal brands into six-figure roles and worked closely with politicians, CEOs, and industry leaders.

☆ Meet Max Orelus, the Job Speed Dater

Max Orelus, one of my coaching clients, has been developing websites since the age of 14. He first started making money online at the age of 16 and at 22, grew what was at the time one of the largest celebrity websites for a single artist, which reached more than 2 million viewers a month. While he lived and breathed tech, jumping into the corporate world was a different story. During his rise as a web designer, he recalls, companies didn't care what you did apart from "real" experience; in other words, sitting in a cubicle for some corporation. Max started at the bottom, the same way as everybody else who had no experience at all. The only difference was that he already had more than eight years of web development under his belt and had already cleared $100,000 in a year without ever getting a "real" job. I spoke with him about how speed dating jobs helped him achieve his career goals.

Q️ *How has speed dating jobs helped you reach your career goals, raise your salary, and expand your professional network?*

A️ Speed dating jobs has cut out the BS corporations try to sell you on. You stop caring about what the company wants first, and you start putting yourself as the prize. You find out quickly whether you are interested in the work you're doing. Plus, who needs a measly 3 percent raise every year when you can go to another company and get 15 to 20 percent? It's a no-brainer. For me, my motives were simple: "You can always achieve something if you've done it before." For me, I've touched $100,000 on my own [working independently], so it shouldn't be too hard in the corporate world.

Q️ *What are some of the best unique experiences and exposure you have gotten from dating jobs?*

A️ Networking. The ability to meet professionals from all walks of life. The most memorable experience was actually connecting with you. We were two young professionals

Max Orelus, continued

working at one of the Big Four. You had just found another position working for some other company, and so did I. I started at this new company with a 22 percent increase to my salary. I was at this company for about a month without getting my essential equipment to actually do any work. I was bored, and I already had an idea of what a mistake I had made. Somewhere down the line after working a month at this new company, I received a phone call from the company that you just started at. To make a long story short, I started at the same company one week later with an overall salary increase of 63 percent. If that's not job speed dating, then I don't know what is!

☆ *What advice would you give to someone who is scared to date jobs as they build their personal brand?*

☆ This is not the world your mom and dad grew up in. Companies used to be the only brand. It doesn't work that way anymore. Every individual is their own brand. You need to care more about *your* brand than the company's brand. You're basically using the same rules that apply to everyday relationships. How can you make someone's brand better when your brand is weak or lacking? You can probably do it, but it's probably not going to make you happy.

Also, do yourself a favor and stick to science, technology, engineering, and mathematics (STEM) if you don't want to be broke in the next 10 to 20 years.

7

☆ ☆ ☆

MARKET YOURSELF LIKE AN AD

Now that you have been working on building your brand, letting go of that employee mindset, and dating jobs, it's time to TEST your career by marketing yourself. If you remember the section on career depression in Chapter 3, you read about flipping the idea of being career SAD (stress, anxiety, and depression) into the idea of looking at yourself as an AD. Since you have solidly established your brand, you can now be ADS, which means you can *accomplish dominating success* for your career.

Within the marketing world, ads help consumers know that brands exist. You see them on TV as commercials, on the internet through social media, and in the windows as you walk past storefronts. These ads persuade people to buy a product or service. You have to be an ad for your brand so career builders and career agents will want to see what you have to offer. A great resume with great experience holds little value if it's not marketed well online. If no one notices you, it will be very difficult for people to connect with you on LinkedIn or email you about your dream job. Remember: You offer education, experience, and expertise that companies need to know about.

You have to prepare for your brand launch, just as you would if you were marketing a product or service. You will need a pre-marketing checklist, marketing strategy plan, and result-gathering process for your brand. As you will learn in this chapter, you can't sell anything you have not marketed to the right people, both in person and online.

The Rehab YOU Pre-Marketing Checklist

When a real estate agent is working with a client who is ready to sell their home, they first have to get the house ready for the market. Before the for-sale sign goes up, the house has to go through home inspection, and some things have to be fixed or renovated. Your career is the same—you just need a different kind of checklist. According to thebalancecareers.com, it takes roughly six months to complete a job search and land a job offer, though that can vary depending on the industry and where you live. It's the same thing with your brand. Before you start marketing yourself like an ad, you have to properly position yourself for the recruiters, diversity inclusion managers, and industry in general. You have to be sure you can tell the story of your brand's education, experience, and expertise. Start by creating your Rehab YOU Pre-Marketing Checklist:

1. *Education.* Add all college degrees, professional certifications, and professional training courses to your resume.

2. *Experience*. Update your professional experience and make sure your current company information, job titles, and duties and responsibilities are accurate.

3. *Expertise*. Sprinkle all the current cutting-edge keywords throughout the resume to display your expertise in various industry-related topics.

4. *Exposure*. Identify where you want to get your marketing exposure online. Make sure you have updated your resume information on sites like LinkedIn, Indeed, CareerBuilder, USAJOBS (if you are seeking federal government jobs), etc.

As soon as your job website profiles and LinkedIn profile have been updated, recruiters, colleagues, and industry leaders will get notifications that you have added a new role, skills, or completed education. This is indirect marketing for your brand. You are allowing the internet to send off your ad to the world before the direct marketing takes place.

The Rehab YOU Marketing Plan

The Rehab YOU Marketing Plan will help you succeed, because it identifies the who, what, when, where, why, and how of marketing your personal brand. This plan gives you clear insight on how to market yourself online. First, define:

- → *Who*: Identify your career marketing audience.
- → *What*: Develop a job search formula.
- → *When*: Determine marketing frequency—how often will you apply for new career roles?
- → *Where*: Identify where you will market yourself for a new career role.
- → *Why*: Understand why marketing your personal brand increases your chances of landing a job interview.
- → *How*: Review your career marketing metrics and marketing tools so you can measure your success.

Let's walk through each of these elements of your marketing plan.

WHO: Identify Your Career Marketing Audience

As you market yourself online, in person, and throughout your current organization, you need to define your primary marketing audience. Sometimes you will meet individuals in person at job fairs, conferences, and networking events or online via social media, so you must learn how to display your education, experience, and expertise during conversations. Always have your resume, online portfolio, and LinkedIn profile updated and ready for your marketing audience, which may include:

→ *College professors.* They can help cool geeks, college students, or recent graduates land internships with an organization.

→ *Professionals.* These may be co-workers, former college classmates, or someone you meet at an event.

→ *Human resources specialists.* The HR team usually resystematizes who performs recruiting and has access to new openings within an organization.

→ *Recruiters.* These are our career agents—they look for professionals with strong brands and reach out to people with outstanding resumes and LinkedIn profiles.

→ *Diversity inclusion managers.* They are responsible for finding talented minorities to support an organization's diversity inclusion efforts.

→ *Industry leaders.* These can include CEOs, CFOs, and vice presidents of organizations; they usually have the power to hire or fire professionals.

All these potential audiences have the social and corporate capital you need to advance your marketing plan. It's up to you to figure out the most appropriate way to interact with each one.

WHAT: Develop Your Career Rehab Job Search Formula

Developing a job search formula will help you maximize your marketing. You can't successfully market yourself if your job search doesn't return enough opportunities to apply to online. I have found that many of my clients tap out on their job search because they don't have an effective search plan or they underuse the filters options on job board websites. I have created a job search formula so you can feel confident in your career marketing plan. I want you to be able to apply to countless jobs in many cities with a good salary range.

Here is the Career Rehab Job Search Formula:

Job Titles + Job Search Filters + Job Applications
= Job Interviews

Let's walk through the three steps that lead to job interviews:

1. *Job titles.* Create a list of 10 to 15 job titles in your industry. If you don't know, you can use Google to search the following: "Job titles that fall under [job type or category]." For example, you could search for "Job titles that fall under project management." Since so many companies use different titles for a project manager position, search for jobs using most or all of these titles listed below:
   - Project manager
   - Senior project manager
   - Assistant project manager
   - IT project manager
   - Project administrator
   - Software project manager
   - Project coordinator
   - Project analyst
   - Project support officer
   - Project office coordinator
   - Project management office (PMO) analyst
   - PMO specialist
   - Portfolio office analyst
   - PMO manager
   - Project planner

2. *Job search filters.* Define the job search filters you will need, depending on where you want to work and how much you want to get paid.

For example:

City, State: Washington, DC

Salary Range: $90,000 to $100,000

3. *Job applications.* From Monday through Friday, take one to two of the job titles in your list and apply to 10 to 20 jobs per day. By the end of the week, you should have applied to 50 or more jobs using LinkedIn, Indeed, Glassdoor, Monster, or CareerBuilder. For example: On Monday use LinkedIn, Tuesday use Indeed, Wednesday use CareerBuilder, Thursday use Monster, and Friday use Glassdoor.

If you consistently follow the Career Rehab Job Search Formula, you will land job interviews. A week or two of applying to jobs is not enough time to properly market your brand if you want to have multiple career options. Remember, finding the right job is like finding the right home to purchase; it can take weeks or months as you search for homes in the right area, and in your price range. It's the same with your job search. You have to be patient because you don't just want any job—you want the right job.

WHEN: Determine Marketing Frequency

In the real estate industry, the summer is a boom time, when lots of home buyers are looking at and purchasing homes. Similarly, during the calendar year, there is a best time for professionals to look and apply for a new job. According to Career Sidekick, the winter months of January and February are great for getting hired in most industries, with the spring months a close second. Since career marketing and job searching are most successful toward the beginning of the year, that's great news for those professionals who believe in New Year's resolutions or who just want to start the year on a good note.

That said, don't be alarmed if you apply to jobs early in the year but don't hear anything back for a few weeks or a month. The HR professionals may still be on holiday vacation, or the interview panel may not all be back on the same schedule to perform the job interview. Patience is key; you can use the wait time to hone and develop your talking points (we'll talk more about interviewing in Chapter 8).

WHERE: Identify Ideal Marketing Locations

In addition to applying to new career roles as you expand your career floor plan, you have to learn to identify where you can best market your education, experience, and expertise. Remember, you are bigger than your resume. You are a personal brand with unique qualities that an organization can benefit from. Most nonprofits, government organizations, and private-sector companies are marketing their offerings the same way you are marketing your personal brand. They often have a LinkedIn company profile, an Indeed company profile, a YouTube channel, a SlideShare profile, a company website, and published white papers. You should have the same online presence for your personal brand. As you see yourself more as a brand, you can begin to identify the most useful platforms to market yourself to recruiters, hiring managers, and colleagues.

Below are ten places you can market your career expertise:

1. *LinkedIn.* Create a profile so you can connect with colleagues, career builders, and career agents; then build your network, push out career-related content, and learn from other industry experts.

2. *Indeed.* Upload your resume to this online job board website so career agents can find you for new opportunities.

3. *SlideShare.* Share your industry-related presentations and technical talks on this online presentation platform. These presentations can also be reshared and marketed on LinkedIn, and you can share your expertise with hiring managers and recruiters.

4. *YouTube.* Interview experts and showcase your industry experience and expertise on this online video platform. Record your live presentations and upload them to your YouTube channel so you can market your expertise and speaking skills.

5. *Website/blog*. Create a website branded with your name and create content related to your industry expertise. You can write blog posts, post your YouTube videos (linking two locations!), and post your professional biography to market your education, experience, and expertise.

6. *White papers*. These are like the book reports or research papers you wrote in college. But in the corporate world, white papers are provided by companies to validate a service or product they offer. As a professional, you can write and publish your own white papers emphasizing your subject expertise in technology, human resources, health care, etc.

7. *Podcasts*. Over the past few years, podcasting has become extremely popular and is a good way to demonstrate your expertise to fellow professionals. If you have a very niche expertise, there probably is a podcast for it. Pitch yourself to the show and see if you can be featured on it as an expert in your industry. Another way to be viewed as a career expert is to host your own podcast, where you can feature other experts or be the featured expert each episode. In other words, you become the gatekeeper.

8. *Books/ebooks*. Publishing a book about a specific career solution, experiment, or practical advice is a very cost-effective way to publicize your industry knowledge. A book can be a game changer for your personal brand because it validates you and positions you as an expert in your industry.

9. *Professional certification badges/signatures*. Adding your certifications to your resume, LinkedIn profile, and email signature is free marketing to recruiters, your current workplace, and hiring managers. Passing professional certification exams is an easy way to let people know that you are a subject matter expert.

10. *Freelance articles*. Volunteering to write professional articles for editorial websites is a great way to market your expertise. For instance, I have written many articles for Glassdoor, where I have shared my career coaching advice with college

students and professionals. Commit to writing one or two articles per month and market them on social media after they are published.

No matter what mix of marketing methods you choose, you can target a variety of markets and audiences who need (and want) to see what you bring to the table. As recruiters, colleagues, and industry leaders review your profile, they can also find related career content you've created that represents your education, experience, and expertise.

WHY: Personal Brand Marketing Matters

The traditional hiring process is becoming obsolete. Within this digital age personal brand marketing really enhances your chance of being noticed online. Also, it helps hiring managers and recruiters find rock star professionals without having to do in-person job fairs all the time. Your personal brand marketing is going to set you apart from everyone else online who desires to land a good paying job. If your personal brand is solid online you will constantly receive emails and phone calls from recruiters.

If you don't have an online presence you are not even in the race. Don't be scared to put yourself out there. You have education, experience, and exposure that the world should know about. It's so important to keep your brand relevant. Brands like Apple, Google and Nike have mastered the art of staying relevant. These brands continue to evolve with the online marketing trends and you should too. You don't want your brand to dissolve—you want it to continue to evolve. Rehab YOU marketing is all about the evolution of your personal brand and career skills.

HOW: Review Career Marketing Metrics

As you market your personal brand, continually assess your marketing strategy by reviewing the results. We all check our personal social media profiles to see how many people liked our Facebook post or viewed our video on Instagram—we have to do the same for our professional profiles. Your marketing metrics will tell you what is working well for your personal brand—and what isn't. As you gather these metrics, adjust your marketing activities accordingly. Follow these five steps:

1. Review your LinkedIn profile views. This will tell you how many people viewed your profile and what company they currently work at. It will also notify you when someone has viewed your job application.

2. Review your Indeed profile views. This will tell you how many times your profile came up on the employee search and how many people viewed your resume.

3. Check your emails to see how many recruiters are contacting you about jobs you may qualify for. As an IT professional, I receive three to six emails a day from company recruiters.

4. Review your LinkedIn direct messages from professionals and industry recruiters. LinkedIn has a direct message functionality where you can send messages to other professionals.

5. If you are sharing information on Facebook, Twitter, Instagram, or YouTube, you should be able to review your content's likes, comments, shares, and reposts. This will help you understand what type of content is connecting with people more.

In this digital age, online marketing is helping professionals maintain their brand outside their jobs. Professionals are either representing their organization or themselves. You have the power to market yourself like an ad, but you have to be consistent and persistent. You should always be looking for new ways to create better content, enhance your marketing plan, and assess your marketing metrics.

☆ Meet Crystal Chisholm, Certified Diversity Recruiter and Personal Branding Strategist

Crystal Chisholm is an author, speaker, professional development trainer, certified diversity recruiter, and personal branding strategist. She is also the CEO of Crayne Career Solutions, which was established in 2016 to deliver personal brand marketing services and workshops for job seekers, career professionals, entrepreneurs, educational institutions, government agencies, nonprofit organizations, and specialized groups. Her book is *Branding Is a Big Deal: How to Identify, Market, and Attract Purpose Driven Opportunities* (Crayne Career Solutions, 2019).

☆ *Why do you think professionals struggle with marketing themselves like an ad for their career?*

☆ This is something that I was challenged with myself for many years and found out that I was not alone. From students to executives, this is just a tough thing for most to do. One of the first questions that I ask my clients during my intake sessions is to describe themselves using three adjectives, but they are often unable to come up with at least two.

I have found the same challenge as a recruiter while interviewing candidates. When asked the question, "Can you describe yourself?" or, "What are some of your leadership qualities?", most struggle with identifying what makes them unique or how they would be an asset to the organization.

I believe that most professionals struggle with marketing themselves like an ad because they lack confidence and self-reflection or they simply just don't know how to do it! Some professionals still subscribe to the idea that traditional methods (write a resume, apply to a job online, and wait for a response or, if internally, wait for a promotion to "fall from the sky") work. Statistics and trends have proven that traditional methods are antiquated and brand content marketing is king.

On the flip side, there are some who would boldly market themselves like an ad but feel like if they market themselves, it is a form of bragging or would cause tension within the workplace, so they choose to avoid it altogether. Minorities, in particular, are usually less vocal about their achievements because we have been stigmatized as aggressive, and combative, and are often told that we are a threat, which

Meet Crystal Chisholm, continued

can lead to stifled career opportunities or termination (very extreme, but it has happened). Therefore, we are expected to remain "humble" and grateful for whatever opportunities are presented to us.

☆ *What are the top three ways people can improve how they execute marketing their personal brand for career enhancement?*

☆ *Conduct a personal SWOT analysis:*

→ *Strengths*. Identify their superpower and in what capacity it has been used. Was it successful? If no, back to the drawing board.

→ *Weaknesses*. What are some things they need to work on, and what's the plan to turn that weakness into a strength?

→ *Opportunities*. What current or future opportunities do they have that could propel them further?

→ *Threats*. Who or what is their competition? Create a plan of action for not allowing it to become a roadblock.

They should use the responses from this SWOT analysis to build or rebuild a powerful brand.

Connect with the movers and shakers online. The best part of social media is the ability to immediately connect and communicate with people from all walks of life worldwide. If a leader or influencer within their industry posts, they should tag and respond to the poster with a response that allows the poster to immediately identify their value or knowledge on the topic of discussion. Although the poster may not immediately notice the response, the job seeker/professional should be consistent in trying to build a relationship and getting their attention. This can help increase their visibility tremendously.

Secure a mentor. Mentors are the ultimate plug because they have been there and done that. Their years of experience, wisdom, and mile-long contact list are pivotal in their exposure and growth.

☆ *If a professional does not want to be on social media or LinkedIn, what marketing options do they have?*

Meet Crystal Chisholm, continued

⭐ As a volunteer career coach for workers 50 years of age and older, I often face this challenge. But I have also seen an increasing number of young adults who are introverted and would rather not be exposed on social media, either. In these cases, I warn them that their journey may be slower, but it will not be dead.

Marketing does not only happen online; it also happens on paper and in person. For brand exposure, they can blog on their topics of choice, either using a site like Medium or a personal blogger website. Some other ideas I'd suggest include:

→ Create business cards and keep them handy to pass out during meetings and networking events.

→ Attend local job clubs and industry-related networking events.

→ Have an updated resume and business cards in hand and/or electronically just in case they are asked to email information over.

→ Create a neighborhood buzz, which includes the mailman, hairdresser, barber, teacher, crossing guard, cashier at favorite coffee shop, etc.

Eventually, word-of-mouth will spread like wildfire and is still very powerful. In fact, a recent recruiting study confirmed that 80 percent of jobs are filled by referrals.

✪ *Other than a resume, cover letter, and LinkedIn profile, what other artifacts can professionals market to increase their personal brand awareness online?*

⭐ Other ways to increase personal brand awareness online could be through these mediums:

→ *Personal website*. Website builders like Wix, Weebly, and GoDaddy have templates that allow even the most novice individuals to create a stunning website.

→ *Social media profiles*. Dedicated to their brand (e.g., an Instagram page dedicated strictly to fashion if in the field of fashion).

→ *Project portfolio*. What better way to show your stuff than to present a portfolio full of creative design work?

Meet Crystal Chisholm, continued

→ *Blog*. Communication is key in any organization, and employers appreciate rock stars who have the keen ability to articulate and convey messages that can help them gain profitability and exposure. The blog should focus on industry-related information to really gain the attention of the interviewer/reader.

☆ ☆ ☆

BE YOU, SELL YOU

The next phase in the Rehab YOU process is all about selling your personal brand as you interview for new roles or for ad hoc opportunities like speaking engagements, side hustles, or consulting gigs. You have already learned how to build your brand by dating jobs and market yourself like an ad. Now it's time to learn how to sell yourself and seal the deal. Once people show interest in your personal brand, you have to make them want to hire you. Your brand can look very attractive on your resume, LinkedIn profile, and social media, but you still have to close the sale in job interviews.

I like to refer to job interviews as a stage, and your performance as showtime. Or, if you prefer, you can think of it as a real estate showing. When a homeowner is ready to sell their home, the real estate agent hosts an open house to show it to potential buyers. Those open houses are like job interviews, and you are the home. You have to impress potential employers the same way the home has to impress a family. Remember, you are a product, and you have to sell yourself in job interviews, whether they're done via phone, video, or in person, and whether you're dealing with one or more individuals.

The art of nailing a job interview with ease lies in making it more conversational. Conversational interviews give you more control over being your true self and selling who you really are. Sometimes being overprepared from a technical perspective keeps your personality from coming through. Most great companies want to see if you are qualified, but they also want to see if you are a good fit for their culture. In this chapter, you will learn how to properly prepare for a job interview and perform well as you interview with panels. Job interviews can be intimidating, but I will teach you how to develop thought-provoking questions for your interviewers that will leave a lasting impression—always helpful for getting job offers!

Preparing for Showtime: The Job Interview

Most traditional career coaches teach you to prepare for a job interview the usual way: Know your resume, research the company, and review the job description. But I like to instruct my clients to tell their brand's story in a way that displays their subject-matter expertise. "Showtime" during the job interview should be you talking about your work experience like it's a movie. Acquaint the interview panel with your education, experience, and expertise in a way that allows them to get to know you as a person, not just as a professional. If you have a special offering or skill set, describe your experience the same way Beyoncé displays her musical skills onstage. Remember, celebrity branding is all about you shining and you will display your career worth when you perform well in job interviews.

When a person is looking for a new home, they want unique community amenities, appliances, and spaces that other homes don't offer. When you show up at a job interview, your goal is to showcase what is unique and special about you. You want to walk out leaving a memorable impression and with the panel feeling like you killed the interview.

When you sell yourself in job interviews, you want to sell your career experiences through storytelling. Use this Job Interview Preparation Checklist to create a winning impression:

❑ Know the story of your personal brand and be able to express it smoothly to the interview panel. They want to know who you are, where you were educated, where you have worked, and where you are going in the future.

❑ Understand the methodologies and technologies listed in the job announcement. Become comfortable with analyzing processes and industry life cycles and back that up with technology implementation.

❑ Describe how you can add value back to the company based on their offerings and mission. When a company offers a service and you have that expertise, explain how your experience, education, and expertise can help move the company forward.

❑ Make sure your personality shines through your responses and questions for the panel. When you show your personal side, this allows you to get a feel for the company culture, and they get to learn about you as well.

Showtime Rehearsal: Practice for the Job Interview

As you prepare for showtime, you can rehearse with the people who can give you the best feedback. It's a great idea to practice with a good friend, spouse, mentor, career coach, or former manager or colleague (if you remain on good terms). Select someone who will give you honest, raw feedback. I always practice my interview skills with my husband. He always critiques my responses, my tech knowledge, and how I deliver my questions to the panel. I encourage you to start preparing for a job interview 72 hours ahead of time so the information will be fresh in your mind.

Don't Bomb the Job Interview

One of most professionals' biggest fears is performing poorly in a job interview. It's not unlike when a home has been on the market for a very long time. The owner starts to feel like their well-loved home is a horrible piece of property. It's the same with us as professionals. But there are good reasons you might bomb a job interview. Some of the most common interview mistakes can include not dressing for the part, having a limited knowledge of the company because you didn't do your research, showing up late, forgetting to bring a hard copy of your resume, and not asking any questions about the company.

Of course, you may be running late through no fault of your own: Maybe a car accident caused a huge, unexpected traffic snarl. Life happens, but it's vitally important to communicate your potential tardiness before you are actually late. Call or email the point of contact to let them know the situation and see if you need to reschedule or if they still want you to come to the interview. Similarly, in this digital age, having a hard copy of your resume is not always necessary, but it's better to be prepared than unprepared. So please bring your resume with you to the job interview.

When it comes to dressing for the interview, always try to dress for the company culture and add a few touches of personality. Don't go over the top, because you want them to focus on your performance, not on what you are wearing. If you don't do the proper research, you may not dress correctly. For example, if you wear a suit to an interview at *Rolling Stone* magazine, it will be obvious that you didn't research the company, because they don't have a conservative culture.

It will be very clear to the interview panel if you don't know anything about the company. Most of the time, the interview panel will give you a brief introduction to the organization, but they want to rate your interest in the company based on what you can tell them about their mission, products, and services. So definitely learn the basics, but also do a deeper dive in your research. Keeping up with the company's new business announcements, blog posts, or clients will help you develop your list of questions for the interview panel. Try to ask them questions that bring that "wow" factor to the conversation.

Most professionals will ask standard questions about their role, the company culture, and career growth. But you want to ask questions that hook into where you can add value or where they are trying to go in the future. These may include:

- → Technical questions about the role and its responsibilities
- → General questions about the company culture, growth, diversity, or work-life balance
- → Wow-factor questions about a current event or business announcement regarding the company's future

Has the company recently been in the news for a new innovation? Ask about it! Today, most companies are looking for creative professionals who can add value. So as you go into your interview, put your innovator hat on and think outside the box as you discuss your interest in the company. Job interviews are an opportunity to win the panel over with your savviness and business-driven ideas. So think about what type of employees companies like Apple, Nike, and Facebook would want representing their brand. You are learning to sell yourself as a fan or advocate for their company brand.

Sell the Resume You or the Real You

Sometimes professionals show up on time, bring a hard copy of their resumes, and dress very well for the job, but their nervousness overtakes them. Their inability to perform well may be because they are trying too hard to sell their resume and not themselves. I know it's hard to distinguish at times. The job interview is a selling exercise and you have to know when you are overselling your resume and when you are overselling your authenticity. To get around that, try using my Rehab YOU Job Interview Formula:

Sell 70 percent of your resume
Sell 30 percent of the real you
= 100 percent success

When you are selling your resume, you are focusing on your education, experience, and expertise. You are telling the story of your personal brand and backing it up with technical knowledge, communications skills, and professional certifications.

Selling the Real Me vs. the Resume Me

As an information technology professional, I have become more comfortable over time with selling the real me, rather than the resume me. Earlier in my career, I loved selling the resume me because I wasn't sure what type of organization was a good fit for my personality. I was more excited about getting a job offer than the right job offer.

My most recent job interview was in 2018, for a senior project manager position with the federal government. I was a little reluctant, because I wasn't sure whether I wanted to return to work while managing my growing business as a career coach. The hiring manager had found my profile on LinkedIn and messaged me, so marketing my personal brand was working. We spoke on the phone, I gave it some thought, and then I interviewed for the role in person. The interview panel included the hiring manager and two other team managers I would be working for.

I was ready for "showtime" when I arrived for the interview. I tried not to focus as much on listing my technical skills, but instead told how I applied those technical skills to real-life projects, and poured my personality into the storytelling so they could learn about the real me. I knew my resume was solid, but I wanted them to know that if you hire me, this is Kanika— and she has a BIG and bright personality. I was asked to sketch out a solution for managing a website content migration project. I mapped it out from A-Z, still selling my personality in every step. Their eyes widened as I performed with high energy. As I left the building and went to retrieve my car from the parking garage, I got a call from the hiring manager offering me the job.

This was new: I had never gotten a job offer within 10 minutes of leaving the interview. I guess my "showtime" performance proved I knew my resume, but also showed I did a good job at selling the real me.

Professionals must always understand that job interviews may require you to problem solve or perform technical analysis, which should be backed up by your resume.

On the other hand, when you sell the real you in your job interview, you do it by being upbeat, smiling, and responding politely. Selling the real you means presenting your best self and displaying your personality (along with all the hard skills the employer is looking for). When a family is selling their home, they are selling the actual features and possible renovations in the home description, which is similar to your resume. But when they are being flexible with the price, offering closing costs, and providing a warm, welcoming experience at the open house, they are selling their personalities. You have to sell yourself the same way in a job interview. Win over their hearts with your personality and win over their minds with your technical expertise.

Other Types of Stages for Job Interview "Showtime"

Job interview formats have changed so much over the years, and many companies are now conducting phone and video interviews. I like to call these "other types of stages" you will have to learn how to perform on. I know what you are probably thinking: *How can I sell myself through the phone if no one can see me?* Just because they can't see you doesn't mean they can't feel your energy.

Sometimes your career agent will reach out to you for a quick phone screening with the interview panel. This is usually your round one interview, and it's a way for companies to eliminate weaker candidates. So always bring your best self to a phone screening interview.

Then comes the next round of interviews, which may be in the form of a video or in-person interview. I have interviewed with companies that only conducted phone and video interviews. It all depends on the bandwidth of the hiring team, logistics, and timeline. But either way, remember you are a brand, so always present your best self on a video interview. I don't recommend getting dressed up in a suit, but you should at least wear business casual and have a good video camera on your computer for a clear image.

Here are some ways to sell yourself in telephone and video interviews:

Telephone

→ If you plan to use a mobile device, always conduct your job interviews in areas that have stable mobile phone service.

→ Dial into the phone interview five minutes in advance and place your phone on mute until the interview starts.

→ Conduct the interview in a quiet place and remove all distractions from the room.

→ Smile as you respond to each question and speak slowly and clearly. Interviewers can "hear" your smile over the phone.

→ At the end of the job interview, thank the panel for taking the time to interview you.

→ Be clear about the next steps once the interview is over.

Video

→ Always use a computer or laptop that has a clear video camera, and place your computer on mute until the interview starts.

→ Use a stable home or work internet connection. Don't use a public wifi connection that may drop in and out.

→ Log into the video conference tool 10 to 15 minutes in advance, just in case you have to download software to your computer.

→ Smile as you respond to each interview question; use the video functionality to show your personality.

→ At the end of the job interview, show your gratitude to the panel for taking the time to interview you.

→ Be clear about the next steps once the interview is over.

Don't treat telephone and video interviews differently than an in-person interview. Make sure you have your questions ready to ask the panel and be on time. If you can't make the interview due to an emergency or scheduling conflict, notify the point of contact or career agent via email or phone immediately. The key to performing well in any job interview is to show up and show out: Bring your real self and resume self to the interview.

Follow Up to Seal the Deal

The best way to seal the deal on a job interview is to follow up within 48 hours. After that point, the interview panel may not remember you if they have spoken with a large number of applicants. It's always best to ask for business cards at the end of the interview if they have not been provided. Use those cards to email the panel, thanking them for their time. Since you are a "wow factor" candidate, you want to continue to display gratitude and strong interest in the position. Even if you feel like you did not do well in the interview, always send a follow-up email, because even though you may think you bombed the job interview, they may think you're the bomb. In the past, I have reused thank-you job interview email templates by adding my own flavor and creating a new sentence structure. The key is to have a boilerplate template that you can use again and again. You can always customize your thank-you email for a specific role; you want to connect with the interview panel. Even if you have more than one round of interviews for the same role, make sure you follow up at the end of each round. You may be interviewing with different people each time, so it's important to keep the momentum going as you kill each interview.

Below are some best practices for sending thank-you emails after interviews:

→ Send the email right away, preferably within 48 hours.
→ Keep your email clear, concise, and short.
→ Make sure you keep it professional and don't write too casually.
→ Email the entire interview panel; don't leave anyone out.
→ Express your interest in the role, reiterating why you are qualified for the job.
→ Include your contact information: phone number, email, links to your work, and a link to your LinkedIn profile.

Remember, even if you don't get the job, keep applying to new roles and always be open to interview even when you are not actively looking. The thank-you email may not always seal the deal, but it will go a long way toward making a good, lasting impression that may prove fruitful later. I truly believe in timing: When you trust the Rehab YOU process, the right role will align with your revamped personal brand. When you get an email that you did not get the job, always reply with one last thank-you email. There may be another role there in the future you will be better suited for. Trust your process, and never give up on finding the right job.

☆ Meet Minda Harts,
Author and CEO of The Memo LLC

Minda Harts is the founder and CEO of The Memo, a career development platform for women of color. She also teaches at NYU's Robert F. Wagner Graduate School of Public Service. She is the author of *The Memo: What Women of Color Need to Know to Secure a Seat at the Table* (Seal Press, 2019), which discusses the challenges women of color face in the workplace and how to overcome them.

☆ *How does one secure their seat for a job offer as they are actively interviewing for jobs?*

☆ It can be tricky trying to navigate securing your seat in a new organization or company while you're still tied to your old seat. There was a point in my career when I was unhappy with my current work environment, yet I was not in a position to exit stage left immediately. I had responsibilities that were required of me, and that meant I needed to continue to perform exceptionally at my current place of employment while I strategically planned for my seat at the next table. In 1943, Abraham Maslow created his famous hierarchy of needs, which I reference for career development. According to Maslow, he said we have five needs: physiological, safety, belonging, esteem, and self-actualization. I allowed myself to think through each level of need and dissect what I was looking for in my next "seat." This isn't just another opportunity for a potential employer to interview me, but in return, I have the opportunity to interview my new employer based on my personal career needs. I didn't want to make the mistake of securing just any seat at any table—I had to be intentional about my next steps. We can't be ambivalent about our careers and the tables we sit at or decide to build. Part of securing your new seat at the table will require you to build a

Minda Harts, continued

multidimensional persona, existing in one work environment while striving to achieve your career goals at another. During this time of transition, we have the unique opportunity to level up in our skill sets via certifications or professional development. We can also learn how to articulate our current skills and how they can be transferrable in new industries. As you are pursuing your next career move, this doesn't have to be a time of career doom and gloom because you aren't in the seat you see yourself in—this is a time to get crystal clear on your career needs and what will better serve you when you secure your next seat.

Q *What is the process of knowing whether a job is a good fit or bad fit as a woman of color?*

A I believe knowing what a good or bad fit is goes back to Maslow's hierarchy of needs. Once we become crystal clear on what success looks like to us and what we need and want out of our careers, then we will know which interview questions to ask during the interview process. Part of finding the right "fit" requires research. Part of your research process will require an internal assessment—understanding our personal wants and needs. We must learn to carve out the time to define what "fit" means to us. For example, I know that one of my basic career needs is esteem. Meaning, I need to receive feedback from my manager(s) and colleagues. I am not able to operate at my career best without feedback. When I am assessing if an environment is a good fit for me, I craft questions that will get to the heart of how my future manager might give feedback. Simply asking the question "What is your managerial style?" will not uncover if my esteem needs will be met by joining this team. But if I ask, "How do you like to give and receive feedback from your direct reports?", it will give me more insight into if my esteem needs will be a good fit or not. You can use this framework with any of the five needs in the hierarchy.

Q *As a woman of color, how do you sell the real you vs. the resume you? How do we sell ourselves (personal brand) without selling out?*

A At my company, The Memo, I established four key values: balance, generosity, integrity, and resilience. And whenever I am in a position where I have to decide, *Am I going to show up as the real Minda or the resume Minda?*, I ask myself to consider if the outcome will align with my values. And if the answer is yes, then I am bringing

Minda Harts, continued

the real me and there is no selling out required. But if I can't say yes, then I have to consider whether selling out is worth it. In my opinion, whether it's in a work setting or a personal setting, you should always bring the real you. Your authentic brand is one that has integrity and vulnerability. Anything outside of your authentic "you" is selling out. Do you want a seat at a table that would require you to sell out?

Some of you might be thinking, *Can I merge the resume me and the real me?* and still be authentic, and the answer is yes. Practice bringing every part of yourself to the table. Securing your seat long term will require all of you. And when your clients and colleagues feel like they have "seen" the true you, they will be able to vouch for you, and the people in your corner wouldn't allow any other version of you to be present.

Perhaps you have straddled the line on who keeps showing up—now is the time to create your core values and decide if selling out is worth it for a few quick wins vs. building a fulfilling and sustainable career based on the real you. I spent over 15 years in the fundraising industry, and whenever I tried to secure funding based on being someone else, I always failed. But when I showed up as myself, that is when I established the most meaningful relationships and impactful deals closed. Always err on [the side of] bringing your full self to the table.

9

☆ ☆ ☆

NETWORK LIKE A HUSTLER

Professional networking is an art that a lot of people take for granted as they build their personal brand, but it's one of the best ways to market and sell yourself into a new job, internship, or business partnership. According to a 2016 survey by consulting firm The Adler Group, around 85 percent of open positions are filled through networking.

Networking is truly worth your time and effort, but some people get overwhelmed at the thought of how to go about it. Earlier in my career,

I loved talking to people everywhere I went, so networking came naturally to me. I guess you could say I have a BIG PERSONALITY. I know everyone does not have my personality, but there are ways you can network like a hustler without changing who you are. Networking should not feel like a task; it should start to get easier even as you get out of your comfort zone.

As you build your career blueprint, plan to be in career spaces and rooms to network with industry leaders, recruiters, and professionals. Most of the time, your career connections are the key to going to the next level in your career. Most professionals are promoted or offered a new job because they already knew someone or they met someone at a professional event: a workshop, happy hour, training class, conference, or party. Networking with new people should always feel casual and never forced, but it is always strategic. As a cool geek, corporate rebel, or career dropout, you should always be thinking ahead about how you can add value to your new career connections or how they can add value to your career. Networking is not a one-way street; it's not all about how you can benefit. Career networking should be more about how you can learn something new from someone or how you can teach them something new. In this chapter, you will learn to navigate networking challenges with a hustler mindset. You will also learn to create your own networking rhythm by identifying what environments you thrive in. By being an active listener when you meet new people, you can see how you can add value to each other's careers. Hustlers network with people they can help, and who can help them build a solid personal brand in return.

What Is a Hustler?

The word "hustler" has a negative connotation these days because of how hustlers have been portrayed in the media, on TV, and in movies. But I think hustlers have genius ways for getting what they want from a new person or situation. The word *hustler*, by definition, means an aggressively enterprising person, or a go-getter. You probably decided to rehab your career because you wanted to be a go-getter. As a personal brand, you are developing an enterprise for your career the same way company brands build enterprises for their products and services. Corporate America is your turf, so hustle yourself into new conversations with people who can help you level up your personal brand or land your dream job.

Check out these four benefits of networking like a hustler:

1. It builds your personal brand confidence because it gives you more opportunities to market and sell your experience, education, and expertise through in-person conversation and online communication.
2. It gives you access to new jobs that you can speed date in the future. As you meet new people, they can help you land a job at the company you've always wanted to work for.
3. It provides more opportunities to exchange information with people who are smarter than you.
4. It encourages you to surround yourself with like-minded professionals and leaders who can support you as you tackle your career challenges.

Networking Mistakes New Hustlers Make

As a rookie networking hustler, you will probably make the same mistakes most of us made when we were starting out. It's OK if you had problems building your network in the past. But try not to make the following four mistakes as a new networking hustler:

1. *Don't overpromote your resume.* Instead, focus on building relationships with your new professional connections. You don't want them to think you're only interested in what they can do for you. If they ask for your resume, then by all means give them a copy. But please don't force it on them; most likely they will review your LinkedIn profile to vet your personal brand and see if it's worth passing your resume on to their hiring manager.
2. *Don't assume someone knows why you are reaching out.* Be clear about why you want to connect with a new person. If you

need help in a certain area, be honest about it, but also be sure to let them know if you can help them in any way.

3. *Don't attend networking events just to collect business cards.* It's vital that you have a short conversation with someone to see if you have things in common. Only then should you ask for their contact information or business card. You want people to remember you and the conversation you had when you reach out at a later time. Make quality career connections, not quantitatively driven ones.

4. *Don't neglect to follow up.* Too often, we get so busy that we forget to follow up after meeting an awesome person at an event or connecting with them online via LinkedIn. Hustlers are proactive and make a huge effort to follow up and follow through.

Hustlers always approach networking with a sense of urgency. Professional networking is a part of their daily life. It's how they create a personal brand and develop a solid foundation of support. The key to networking like a hustler is consistency; doing it on a regular basis helps your network grow stronger.

Network with Those You Know First

When you hear the phrase "network like a hustler," you may think you have to connect with people you've never met. We all know that can be scary, but we also seem to neglect the people we already know. Networking means maintaining a relationship with your family, friends, co-workers, and classmates. It goes beyond the first time you meet someone, requiring you to stay in touch with like-minded professionals online and in person. When I am looking for a new role or trying to learn something new in the IT industry, I reach out to my existing network. The foundation of our relationship has already been established and they know my personal brand, so the process of marketing and selling myself is easier to execute.

Some of the best hustlers know how to get what they want from their existing contacts. I always get in touch with the co-workers who have already passed the IT certifications I am attempting to study for or the professionals I used to work with who are now at companies where I would love to work. I connect with them by first asking how they have been doing, personally and professionally. Always ask people about themselves first, and then ask for the information you need. People love to talk about their personal life and professional accomplishments. Then I talk to them about referring me into their company system for a job I found online, or I simply ask if their company is hiring. Win their hearts over first; then pick their brains.

Most professionals spend too much time applying to jobs that hundreds of other people are vying for, when they should be maximizing their existing networks. When we are too prideful to ask our network for help, we are holding ourselves back from our dream job or useful information that could help us pass a professional certification. Networking hustlers should always see the importance of reconnecting with their professional network. The same way businesses build partnerships with each other, you must build alliances with the professionals, family members, and friends in your network. Hustlers build enterprise networks based on a diverse set of relationships. Individuals within your current network can help you with the following issues:

→ You can always ask a co-worker, classmate, mentor, or manager if you can list them as a professional reference on a job application or resume for a new role.

→ Asking a college professor, professional, mentor, or manager for a letter of recommendation for a job you are applying to always helps your job application look more marketable.

→ A referral for a job is one of the easiest ways to get a new role when you already know professionals who can refer your resume into their company's system.

→ Asking your peers or industry leaders who know a new industry standard, technology, or certification for help is a great way to enhance your knowledge or pass a professional exam.

Your current network is one of your more valuable resources, so make sure you tap into it on a regular basis. It's OK to check in with family and friends, former co-workers, or people you attended college with. Networking is not all about meeting new people; it's also about fostering existing relationships. You never know what someone can do for you or you can do for someone else. Stay connected; good communication is the heart of networking.

Hustlers Network Online

In this digital age, networking online is very easy to implement. We all spend ample time on social media or the internet viewing websites and profiles of people who won't add any value to our career. The key is using the internet strategically to maximize your online networking experience.

You can use the following tools to build your network and expand your knowledge:

→ *Social media.* You can connect with and learn from other professionals using Facebook, Twitter, Instagram, LinkedIn, YouTube, etc. Concentrate on the social media profiles of professionals in the same industry as you or in the industry you desire to get into.

→ *Virtual events.* You can attend professional virtual events, Facebook Live events, and webinars to learn from industry leaders and connect with like-minded professionals. Connecting with attendees is crucial, because they may be able to share new information with you or they may work at a company you have been wanting to apply to.

→ *Online learning platforms.* You can enroll in online courses at sites like Udemy or LinkedIn Learning, where you can connect with other professionals who have taken the course and ones who have left a course review. Introduce yourself to them by sending them a private message within the online learning tool or just connect with them on LinkedIn.

➡ *Blogs/websites.* On the personal websites or blogs of professionals, industry leaders, and authors, you can learn more about their personal brand, expertise, and contact information. Websites and blogs are a great way to contact someone through the contact form or with their email address.

Hustlers Network in Person

My absolute favorite form of networking is in person, because it's a great way to make an emotional connection and an opportunity to identify if they can help you or you can help them. Hustlers who learn how to network in person will become unstoppable because they will master the art of selling themselves to strangers, co-workers, and classmates. So when I say, "Sell yourself," I really mean you will learn how to make connections and foster relationships with people from all walks of life. As you meet new people at work or at an event and hear more about their expertise and background, always have your hustling networking antenna tuned in so you can make a mental or written note to connect with them later. Let's break down the various hustling scenarios:

➡ *Workplace.* Your job should be one of the first places you begin to build your professional network. When you start at a new job, think about who you should connect to, based on your career goals, and schedule networking coffee chats, lunch dates, and solid office conversations. These interactions help you develop a professional relationship with your co-workers, managers, clients, and stakeholders. They need to get to know your personality, professional background, and common interests.

➡ *Professional events.* You will meet some truly awesome people at professional workshops, conferences, and job fairs. You may not always be able to connect with your internal team, so when you attend events, introduce yourself to new people during the breaks, lunch, and when you first arrive at the table. It's also a great idea to attend job fairs, as getting your resume in front of hiring managers and recruiters in person helps you sell yourself faster than trying to do it online.

→ *Personal/social events.* It may feel awkward at times talking about where you work or what you do at personal and social events, but you may meet new people who can add value to your job search. These events are more relaxed, so you can be more transparent about your career needs and more easily pass on information to someone else. When you network like a hustler, you have to use your intellectual swagger to win people over, and personal and social events are often the best atmosphere for that.

→ *Colleges/educational institutions.* We all attend professional training at some point; some of us even go back to college while we are working. No matter where you are in your education or training, connecting and exchanging contact information with your classmates is a good start. If you are in a class with people who are developing personal brands similar to yours, or if you have an awesome instructor with a personal brand you admire, connect with them immediately. Deans, professors, and instructors are a key part of your professional network because they can always teach you something new about your industry and they may know industry leaders who are hiring.

Network Like an Introvert

If you are an introvert and you don't want your communication style and socializing skills to stop you from networking like a hustler, the great news is that it won't. The bad news is that you will have to learn new ways to strategically network at your comfort level, and sometimes you may need to extend yourself a bit. As an introverted hustler, you will have to create a strategic networking plan that will focus on quality over quantity. Your few new high-quality connections online and in person could be all that you need. So don't overthink your plan. Just focus on taking small steps toward your career networking goals.

Introverts are usually the shy, quiet, and calm individuals in the room, so networking does not always come naturally to them. Introverts may actually have an advantage over extroverts in one way, because they are very observant, active listeners, unlike extroverts, who may love to socialize and talk to new people in overcrowded atmospheres. Here are some of the best ways for introverts to network:

→ Learn to be yourself even if it feels uncomfortable, because as you meet new people, they want to get to know the real you.

→ Use LinkedIn or your personal website to ensure you are connecting with the right people online who can help you with your career goal or job search.

→ Focus on attending small, intimate networking events so you don't get overwhelmed.

→ Try to connect with the most important stakeholders first: keynote speakers, event hosts, speaking panels, and hiring companies.

→ Bring an extroverted friend or co-worker to a networking event with you. They will be your networking cheerleader to help you extend yourself.

Introvert hustlers need to learn to listen to their instincts and attempt to sell and market themselves without being scared or shy. I know it won't always be easy, but with practice it will improve over time. Introverts have to get out of their own way and push themselves to attend more, and more diverse, events. Start small, and continue to network up.

Network Like an Extrovert

When you network like an extrovert, be mindful of your actions at events and online. At times, extroverted hustlers can make their networking experience about them. Remember that career rehab networking is a two-way street; it is as much about you helping others as it is about others helping you. Extroverts are usually great at attending events and using LinkedIn and social media to meet other professionals, but their approach must have the clear intention to foster a healthy networking relationship.

Extroverts are usually known as the go-getters in the room, the movers and shakers who network with a purpose. Extrovert hustlers love talking, enjoy getting attention, and are always inspired by others' accomplishments and ideas. These qualities would seem to be an asset for someone who is looking to rehab their career, but they could kill a career networking experience if they come off as cocky. Here are some of the best ways for extroverts to network:

→ Serve as a keynote speaker, panelist, or presenter so you can help others and meet new people who can learn from you.

→ Don't oversell your professional experience and education during online and in-person conversations.

→ Try to do more active listening; don't make the conversation all about what you need or how you feel.

→ Don't focus on how many new people you meet. Instead, concentrate on creating quality networking connections.

→ Attend quality networking events. Don't try to attend every event that is advertised, because not every event will align with your personal brand. Be OK with going to both events that are brand new and those that have had past successes.

Extrovert hustlers can seem like the happiest professionals in the work force, so marketing and selling their personal brand comes easily to them. They just need to focus on enhancing their listening skills so they don't miss vital information. You don't want to rub people the wrong way by attempting to create self-centered networking relationships. Always make sure you conduct networking with purposeful intent as you rehab your career.

Networkers Run the World

Whether you desire to be a business owner or a corporate professional, you are only as good as your network. The networkers of the world run our work force and businesses across the world. Networkers are determined to connect with the right people to push their careers and businesses forward. If you want to do the same, try to network with people who can add value to your career, business, and life. Don't forget to add value to others' businesses, careers, and lives while you're at it. The more you network, the more advantages you will have.

☆ Meet Darrell E. Dreher, Jr., Networking Hustler

My client Darrell E. Dreher Jr. is a senior technical account manager in the federal space for Microsoft. Prior to joining Microsoft, he worked for a small systems integrator supporting the Navy. He started as a help desk technician and worked his way up to a program manager in five years, supporting and leading numerous enterprise projects while managing more than 25 resources. Before getting his start in IT, he was a special education teacher for five years in Prince George's County and the District of Columbia school system.

Before you started working at Microsoft, what did you do to build your professional network?

I am always in search for mentors/stakeholders that I could learn and grow from. I often use the term "board of directors." It is always important to have a board of directors for your life that can help advise and guide you along your professional and personal journey. I reached out and looked up to people in my work space that had positions or job functions that I thought were cool. I would always look to dialogue with them and observe from a distance. I also started using LinkedIn as a tool to build my network and connect with recruiters. I would attend networking events and numerous other career fairs to help grow and build my network. I also linked up with you, my longtime friend and career coach

Explain how you utilized your professional network to land a job at Microsoft. What type of networking events did you attend?

I invested in revamping my resume through Kanika's company. I started using LinkedIn as my tool to network with various people and HR resources in my field. I also invested in the premium version of LinkedIn, which allowed me to direct message recruiters. This really opened up doors because I was able to target recruiters for

Darrell E. Dreher, continued

specific jobs I was interested in. In many cases, I was able to follow up with emails, private messages, and phone calls. I had no idea the breadth of jobs Microsoft had available, especially supporting federal customers. I didn't know anyone who worked at Microsoft, so I knew it would be a long process filled with many ups and downs. It was through LinkedIn that I was able to connect with a Microsoft recruiter. Through that recruiter, I saw a posting for an open house for cleared resources at Microsoft. I knew that this would be a great opportunity, I made sure I was dressed properly, prepared with several resumes, and ready to engage in conversation with the hiring team.

Q: Since you have been working at Microsoft, what do you do weekly or monthly to keep your professional network fresh and constantly expanding?

A: I always look to connect with professionals who have similar aspirations. It is also important to continue to grow my LinkedIn network and my network within my company. I never think I am too small or too big to connect with people. I believe we can learn and grow from everybody that we meet. I continue to seek mentors as well as mentor other individuals that are looking to transition and grow their career.

Q: What advice would you give professionals who want to land a job at Microsoft, but they don't know anyone that currently works for the company?

A: Microsoft is a company that is continuously evolving. I think it is important to learn a few technologies that Microsoft specializes in. Use LinkedIn to find people that work for the company, and don't be afraid to connect. The mobile app allows you to connect without a justification for the connection unlike the web app. Reach out to grow your board of directors, and pick their brain. Sometimes it takes buying a cup of coffee or buying lunch in order for that sit-down to take place. Lastly, do not take no for an answer, keep grinding, and keep the faith. Don't be afraid to revamp, make changes, and adjust to ensure you are aligning yourself with your ideal position and career path.

GET PAID NOW: MONEY, POWER, AND RESPECT

As you network like a hustler, you also have to get the money, power, and respect like a hustler. Some of my favorite hustlers are Warren Buffett, Jay-Z, Sean Combs, Oprah Winfrey, Mark Zuckerberg, Brené Brown, and Serena Williams. They all come from different backgrounds, but they have all developed personal brands that incorporate money, power, and respect. As their personal and company brands evolved, they probably rehabbed them several times as they built their career blueprints, learned how to network like a hustler, and speed dated various business opportunities. Whether you are a cool geek, corporate rebel, or career dropout, you too deserve money, power, and respect.

Let's be real. No one is building their brand through education, experience, and expertise to get paid pennies. Everyone wants to get paid more money, and even when they think they are getting a high salary, they may not realize they are being lowballed in other areas. Getting paid should not always be about the money as an end goal. A solid personal and company brand should always want money, power, and respect so they can leverage themselves into better career opportunities for the long term. We all know celebrities, politicians, and athletes who are rich, but may not always get the power and respect they desire. We also all know professionals who may be earning high salaries, but have no power over their careers and their manager does not respect them. But money plus power plus respect makes your personal brand unstoppable.

As a fan of hip-hop music, I always loved how it understands the importance of getting these three things if you want to establish your credibility. Within the urban community and the hip-hop world, it's called "street cred." In this chapter, I'm going to walk you through how to get the money, power, and respect you deserve by building your street cred.

Street Credibility vs. Corporate Credibility

According to Macmillan Dictionary, "street cred" means "respect or admiration among young fashionable people, especially in a city." As I examined this definition, I was amazed at how we as professionals either seek corporate credibility or attempt to build it the same way people do in urban environments. Most people in urban communities are seeking validation from their peers or people who are beneath them in the social pecking order. In urban communities, individuals who have street cred have nice cars, clothes, and a strong influence over how people think and feel. This is similar to the corporate world, where professionals look up to industry leaders and their managers for their accomplishments, salaries, or job titles.

As a cool geek right after college, I wanted a good-paying job as a software developer. Money was the main thing that validated my success then, since I had worked hard for my degree. Then, as I became a corporate rebel with more than seven years of professional work experience, I wanted managers to give me more power to make decisions. I thought having more power in the workplace would enhance my corporate credibility. Then, within the past five years as a career dropout, as an entrepreneur and career coach I wanted people to respect my 14 years of IT experience and career coaching advice. I have learned so much over the years about the concept of "credibility:" We are seeking it from other people when it should come from ourselves.

Corporate credibility, though, is about you validating your marketability by selling yourself into new opportunities. You did the work, developed new skills, and expanded your network. But always remember self-credibility starts with YOU clapping for yourself. Too often, professionals seek outside validation and start to lose sight of what they want for themselves, because they are focusing on what they think others want for them. Hustlers like the influencers I mentioned at the beginning of this chapter have developed their credibility by focusing on and accomplishing their career goals. They all knew what they wanted and they knew their worth. As professionals, we have to know our worth if we want to get paid fairly and treated equally at all times. You are not rehabbing your career to get lowballed and disrespected. You are doing it to create limitless opportunities for your personal brand. That's what corporate credibility is all about.

Money: Know Your Worth

For some professionals, asking for more money is a touchy subject. Most professionals feel validated simply when they get a job offer. But when you don't see yourself as just an employee but as a brand, you will always know your career worth. The best way to define your career worth is by getting the salary and benefits you feel you deserve.

When I interviewed for IT roles, I viewed myself much like an all-star athlete, a Grammy Award-winning musician, or an Emmy Award-winning actress, since I had worked hard to earn my college degree and certifications and to become an industry expert through challenging career experiences. Salary counteroffers were normal in my industry. They're almost like a bidding war—musicians, actors, and athletes negotiate for more money when they sign contracts, and career professionals should do the same. If you know your worth, you can take steps to get the money you deserve.

Don't Get Lowballed

Most professionals focus mainly on their annual base salary when negotiating their job offers, but there are a few other ways to get the money you deserve. Women and minorities are usually lowballed compared to white men in most industries. According to "The Top 10 Facts About the Gender Wage Gap," a 2016 report from the Center for American Progress, "In 2014, the most recent year for which data are available, full-time, year-round working women's annual median wages were $39,621 compared with $50,383 for men." So it's vital to verify that you are getting a fair offer package before you take on a new job. You don't want to accept a job offer and later find out you could be earning a much higher salary.

You can always negotiate the following monetary incentives in your job offer package. Here are five ways to get more money in the deal:

1. *Annual base salary.* In most cases, aim for a $10,000 to $15,000 pay increase when you are interviewing for new roles.
2. *Paid time off (PTO).* You will earn PTO hours each pay period. With your experience, you may be able to get a few more hours per pay period. For instance, if most new employees earn six hours per pay period, see if you can get eight or nine hours instead.
3. *Annual training budget.* Always ask if the company pays for professional training classes each year. This will save

you money on training that will help enhance your personal brand.

4. *Performance bonuses.* Some organizations offer a performance bonus structure that gives high-performing professionals a monetary bonus.

5. *Relocation costs.* Companies that have larger hiring budgets can pay relocation fees for new hires when they are moving from another state for the job. This is awesome because it can cover packing your items, the cost of moving your household and your vehicle, unpacking your items at the other end, real estate transaction costs, and turning on your utilities.

In the real estate industry, websites like Zillow and Trulia offer home listings and property resale values. These tools have become very popular with home buyers and sellers, because they provide good estimates of how much their home is worth or how much a home will cost. Similarly, as a professional you have your own worth when you are looking for a new job or evaluating a job offer. Some of the top salary comparison tools, according to FitSmallBusiness, are Indeed, the Bureau of Labor Statistics, Salary.com, PayScale, and LinkedIn Salary.

Check these out to compare what you are earning now with what you want to earn. With all the work you are putting into building your personal brand, it's so important to use salary comparison tools so you won't get lowballed. These tools are free, and they will always help when you have to negotiate your salary. With your new branding mindset, always know your worth, even if you have to research it. Most celebrities and athletes won't accept a contract without doing their research and comparing it to their performance metrics. You must do the same so you can get a fair annual salary or hourly rate.

Ask for What You Deserve

Remember, you have already validated your corporate credibility by building a solid personal brand. It's time to get the pay you deserve.

But even after using salary comparison tools, most professionals still don't feel comfortable asking for more money. Glassdoor reports that 60 percent of women and 48 percent of men believe salary history questions should not be asked. Women are also less likely to negotiate compensation, and 68 percent of women do not negotiate pay, compared to just around 52 percent of men.

Don't let your age, gender, or race dictate your counteroffer. Pay should be based only on your professional qualifications. If you are interviewing for a company and you feel you are not getting a fair job offer, then the company probably does not value diversity and equality in general. One way to make sure you're getting what you deserve in an offer is to validate the key deal points before you counter. Here are four ways to validate your job offer:

1. *Location.* The cost of living where you are located increases or decreases your annual salary.
2. *Years of professional experience.* The length of your career will measure whether you deserve a junior or a senior-level salary.
3. *Professional certifications.* The number of professional certifications you hold determines whether you qualify as an expert.
4. *Education.* Your college degrees always add value to your expertise as a professional.

When you know your worth in those terms, you will be willing to walk away from job offers that don't make sense. Professionals who really have strong corporate credibility are willing to pass up a lowballed job offer, because they have respect for their own personal brand. They have career power, and they know they control their career trajectory. We as professionals have to take control of that power and make sure we always get equal pay and monetary incentives in a job offer package.

Power: Career Control

Some professionals may have multiple job offers on the table; this is a powerful advantage when making a counteroffer. The best way to get the pay you deserve is to let the company you really want to work for know you have received another offer with a better salary and benefits. At this point, because you have options, the power is in your hands, and you can leverage for extra incentives.

I once interviewed for a well-known consulting company at the same time I was interviewing for their competitor. These two Fortune 500 companies are the Nike and Adidas of consulting firms, and they were always looking to bring in senior consultants like myself at the time. That kind of career control empowers you to ask for what you want in a job offer. As an IT expert with more than 10 years of experience, I expressed high interest in both companies by negotiating not only my salary, but also asking for more PTO and a greater annual training budget. The experience helped me confirm my worth. I began to rely on my power, and I was finally in control of my career.

Don't Give Up Career Power

Even if a company declines your counteroffer, don't feel powerless. There is also power in saying, "No, I am not interested in the job." You are showing the company that you value your experience, education, and expertise over an unfair job offer. Your career power lies in knowing you can get a role with the right pay, benefits, and incentives elsewhere. Trust the negotiation process. Don't negotiate out of desperation, or employers will try to take advantage of you. Just like athletes and actors win contracts to play for a team or star in a movie, you need to negotiate from a place of power. Here are four tried-and-true ways to do that:

1. Decline a job offer after a potential employer doesn't accept your salary counteroffer.
2. Negotiate other benefits, like more work-from-home days or PTO. If you can't get paid more, you can always work from home to save time on your commutes and travel expenses.
3. Counteroffer with a job offer from another company. It's important to show how marketable you are and that other

companies are willing to give you the money, power, and respect you deserve.

4. Allow your recruiter or headhunter to work on your behalf as you negotiate your job offer. Work closely with your recruiter because they can attempt to win over the company. Empower them to do their job.

Career power is more than getting everything you desire in a job offer. It's about knowing you deserve respect. When hustlers like Oprah, Jay-Z, Warren Buffett, and Mark Zuckerberg earned more career power, people gave them more respect. They may have even demanded it sometimes. For example, instead of Oprah Winfrey creating new TV shows and movie productions on an existing media network company, she decided to create her own network. In 2011, the Oprah Winfrey Network (OWN) launched the American specialty television channel jointly owned by Discovery, Inc. and Harpo Studios. According to *TV by the Numbers*, OWN is available to approximately 81.9 million pay television households (70.3 percent of households with TV) in the United States. Career power helps you create opportunities for yourself or through the use of your network. Oprah utilized her career power through the use of her partnership with Discovery, Inc. and her already established company Harpo Studios to build her own television channel.

Respect: Demand It

In the urban community, they say first you get the money, then you get the power, and then you get the respect. This applies to street cred and corporate cred hustlers, too. But respect is not always given; some believe it must be earned. I think respect should be *learned.* No matter what, people must learn early on to respect one another on all career levels. If you are a cool geek, corporate rebel, or career dropout you deserve the same amount of career respect. But it's obvious that as you accomplish more in your career, the better chance you will have to earn respect.

Don't Let Anyone Disrespect You

Too often, professionals allow the hiring team or recruiters to disrespect them or discredit them because of their lack of experience. When interviewing for a role as you continue to rehab your career, you must evolve to a place where you have strong career confidence that no one can break. To do that, follow my quick list of ways you can (and should) demand career respect:

→ Know your workplace rights, labor laws, and HR policies.
→ Correct other professionals when they attempt to disrespect you.
→ Be clear about your pay expectations with recruiters, HR personnel, specialists, and hiring managers.
→ Always give respect during the hiring process; career respect is a two-way street.

If you want to get the pay you deserve, build a respectable personal brand that stands out from all the other professionals you're competing against. Remember: a successful salary counteroffer equals MONEY, POWER, and RESPECT. It's OK to present counteroffers and reject job offers. Rejecting a job shows recruiters that they did not see your career value. Your career salary should always be overvalued unless you are getting other incentives that mean more to you, like work-life balance and training development.

☆ Meet Arquella Hargrove, CEO of Epic Collaborative Advisors

Arquella Hargrove brings a successful 25-year track record of creating and implementing productivity-inducing practices through the application of strategic planning and organization development in both the public and private sector. She has supported both established organizations and entrepreneurial ventures advising through them their stages of creation, growth, and stabilization. As the CEO of Epic Collaborative Advisors, she helps business leaders build stronger, more effective teams and companies. Arquella is a sought-after facilitator, business consultant, speaker, and coach dedicated to the transformative and

Arquella Hargrove, continued

sustainable results of business leaders. She is a moderator and frequent panel speaker in the areas of communication, diversity, human resources management, women in leadership, and social capital, and is a contributor to publications such as Girl Boss Blog and *Workforce* magazine. Arquella holds a bachelor's degree in Human Resources Management from Ottawa University and an Executive MBA from Texas Woman's University.

Q: *How do professionals change their mindset around being more comfortable asking for more money, company benefits, or incentives?*

A: The saying goes, if you don't ask for what you want, then you will not receive it. Or, as my grandmother would say, a closed mouth will not be fed. If we can change our mindset, then we can change our life. I believe that everything we need or want starts with a thought in our mind. Therefore we have to shift the way we think. If you are thinking about a pay increase and how you would benefit from it, but never say anything, then you may continue to receive the standard 3 to 5 percent merit increases or just the COLA—cost of living adjustment. Those increases are never enough for survival. Sometimes the thinking is, *If I ask for more money or benefits, then I may be terminated. If I ask for more then my boss may think all I care about is money and not about my job. If I ask for more, then I will be laid off first because I now make too much money. If I ask for more . . .* and the list of excuses goes on.

The mindset shift change is that I deserve more because I have the experience, knowledge, and skills, and [I am] meeting and exceeding my accomplishments. I will ask for more, and if I don't receive it, then I will be prepared to seek other opportunities.

As long as you work for an organization, you will probably not be paid what you are truly worth. With that in mind, be prepared to do your homework. This means going to sites like Glassdoor, Salary.com, or PayScale. Here, you will check the salary range for your position or the desired position.

As you are requesting to ask for more, be prepared to offer something in return, like another duty and/or responsibility to your workload.

Be prepared with your list of accomplishments, which is valuable to show how you are meeting objectives and helping the company. Managers like seeing the numbers linked to your accomplishments.

Arquella Hargrove, continued

Be prepared with questions and to receive feedback—good, bad, or indifferent.

Finally, be prepared with a plan B, C, and D in case it does not work out in your favor.

The goal is to have the confidence and courage to ask for more with all of your supporting data.

Maya Angelou said it well: If you ask for what you want, be prepared to get it.

Q What advice would you give to women who are scared to ask for more money?

A We already know by reading the data and for some of us working in the area of HR that women are paid less than men in many instances. I suggest that you:

Know how much you want to earn. Before you even think about negotiating salary, it's important to know how much you want to earn. Do the research. Again, check out sites like PayScale, Glassdoor, Salary.com. The purpose is to check what the market range is for your current position or the position you are aspiring to move into at a later date.

Know that it's OK to ask. I do not know many women who are comfortable asking for money and not a raise. You may not feel comfortable asking for more money, but that doesn't mean it's not OK to ask. Find the strength to ask the question rather than wonder if you could have negotiated a better offer. Men do it all day every day. They may not have the full qualifications, but they will still ask for the job or salary increase. And you probably guessed right—90 percent of the time, they receive it.

Be aware of gender differences. It is very prevalent now to see so many articles around the pay differences between men and women. Do your research to understand certain career positions and the salaries linked to them, and if women may traditionally be paid less. If they are, there may be a chance to get more. Be inspired when countering. If the base salary isn't negotiable, perhaps bonuses, benefits, or a commitment for a future raise may be. I have accepted counters that included additional vacation, parking spots (yes, parking is a premium in some places), training courses, etc. Think outside the box and ask for it.

Seek out an ally. Sometimes your manager or someone else in a senior leadership role can be your ally for a better offer. If they want to hire you and see the value, then they will partner with human resources and/or management to get you more money.

Arquella Hargrove, continued

Consider this approach in your inquiry: "I would be ecstatic with the new position, and want to ask about additions to the compensation package." There is no direct ask, only inquiring at this time.

Be prepared to toot your horn. You can share the data you have collected, remind the hiring manager of your credentials, and reiterate your ability to help the organization succeed.

Plan your ask. There are good ways—and not so good ways—to ask for more money.

Be optimistic. When the offer is much lower than you anticipated, stay calm and keep any negative thoughts to yourself. If it's so low that you know you won't take it, it's fine to mention that the offer wasn't what you expected. At that time, you decide if you stay or look for another opportunity.

Q *What advice would you give minority men and women who find out they were lowballed or treated unfairly when it came to equal pay? How should they handle it?*

A Keep your cool at all times is the first thing. If someone is lowballed or treated unfairly when it comes to equal pay, then be sure to have your research ready. Following are some points to consider:

Do your research to confirm the salary disparity and your experience relative to the position.

Once you complete the research, request a meeting with your leader and/or human resources. You can start the meeting by stating, "Thank you for taking the time to meet with me regarding this sensitive matter. It has come to my attention that my pay is not aligned with the market and/or with my counterparts in like positions. Based on my research and experience, I believe my salary should be the same as my counterparts." During your research and meetings, be sure to keep in mind the industry and size of the company. If the company is less than 50 people, then the salary may be slightly different than if it was a larger company. If it is nonprofit, then the salary will not be the same as a for-profit, so be realistic in your salary expectations.

If they agree after your meeting, be sure to request something in writing. If there is no agreement, then decide your next steps for your career projection, knowing you are not receiving the right compensation.

Arquella Hargrove, continued

⭐ *Can you briefly explain the HR policies, laws, and rights employees have when it comes to equal pay, workplace discrimination, Equal Employment Opportunity (EEO) issues, etc.?*

⭐ It is everyone's right to receive fair, equitable pay and to be treated with dignity, respect, and fairness in the workplace. Workplace policies establish boundaries, guidelines, and best practices for acceptable behavior within a company. According to the EEOC, "The right of employees to be free from discrimination in their compensation is protected under several federal laws, including the following enforced by the U.S. Equal Employment Opportunity Commission: the Equal Pay Act of 1963, Title VII of the Civil Rights Act of 1964, the Age Discrimination in Employment Act of 1967, and Title I of the Americans with Disabilities Act of 1990.

"The law against compensation discrimination includes all payments made to or on behalf [of] employees as remuneration for employment. All forms of compensation are covered, including salary, overtime pay, bonuses, stock options, profit sharing and bonus plans, life insurance, vacation and holiday pay, cleaning or gasoline allowances, hotel accommodations, reimbursement for travel expenses, and benefits."

If an employee of a company believes that they are being discriminated against based on pay or any protected class status, then report to human resources. If there is no internal resolution and there are still issues, then you have a right to file a complaint with the EEOC.

⭐ *Lastly, what are other ways professionals can acquire career control (power) and career respect in the workplace?*

⭐ In order for professionals to have control and respect in the workplace, there are some written and unwritten rules that should be followed.

Be on time to work and meetings. If you constantly show up late, then no one will take you seriously and you can miss out on opportunities. Try to arrive 10 to 15 minutes before the start time.

Have a great attitude. No one wants to be around someone who is not so nice all the time. The key to elevation and promotion is about relationships. Be mindful of your

Arquella Hargrove, continued

emotions and manage them accordingly, so people are not trying to avoid you like the plague.

Dress to impress. Be mindful of the way you dress and that it's appropriate for the company environment. Follow the dress code policies if applicable. If there are no policies, then try to dress like the position you want (hopefully in leadership).

Don't let your mouth get you in trouble. Be mindful of your language in the workplace if you want to be taken seriously.

Stay professional at all times. No one wants to hear about your life story, so keep your personal stories to a minimum in the workplace. It's okay to share something about yourself, so people can get to know you and relate. Don't overshare.

Take ownership and be accountable. If you make a mistake or said the wrong thing, own it. Be responsible for your work product and/or service.

Be a resource to others. Be willing to help others and provide any assistance needed. It's not always about you, but the opportunity to help a fellow co-worker or friend speaks volumes and will elevate you to the next level. The Word states, "Give and it shall be given unto you."

11

☆ ☆ ☆

BREAK UP WITH JOBS: FEARLESS RESIGNATIONS

Throughout your career rehab journey, you will date and break up with jobs. I like to refer to the breakups as "fearless resignations." Sometimes a workplace's familiarity delays the process of actively looking for a new job as you prepare for the breakup. It's like you're dating someone you know isn't a good match, but you don't have the courage to say, "This relationship isn't working anymore."

The word "fearless" is very important, because as you build your personal brand, begin to market it online, and sell it in job interviews, your resignations must become fearless. You can't network like a hustler if you're scared to break up with a job you don't enjoy. Resignations are healthy, and part of the Rehab YOU process. There will be times you take a job thinking you will love it, but once you start working there, you realize that the role, workplace, leaders, or company culture is not a good fit. That's when it's time for a breakup.

Breaking up with jobs is similar to telling your real estate agent you no longer want to work with them. It's clear when your agent is not doing their job to get your home sold or find the right home for you to buy. Similarly, you will always know when you are not getting what you need from an organization. Never lose sight of what's in it for you—this is how you remain fearless.

You should always resign in a respectful and professional manner, but your company obviously may not be happy about the breakup. When good employees decide they are ready to leave, some leaders don't know how to handle the idea of you leaving. The first thing they think about is who is going to do your work. It's the same concept when we break up with someone: There could have been signs for months that the relationship was not working, but the other person is still afraid of being alone. However, being emotionally present in a relationship outweighs the physical presence.

In the workplace, organizations should always want professionals who are emotionally committed to the job. When that connection disappears, they become a corporate rebel or career dropout. In this chapter, I'll walk you through how to resign without fear so you can focus on your career renovations.

Why Career Breakups Happen

Let's go back to the comparison to why people fire their real estate agent and look at it a little deeper. According to personal finance website The Balance, some of the top reasons sellers decide not to work with a real estate agent include:

→ Poor communication skills
→ Slow responses to requests

→ Unprofessional behavior

→ Failing to listen to the seller

These are similar to the reasons why professionals resign from a job. According to The Balance Careers website, some of the top reasons employees quit their job are all about the employer. Employers don't always support the career goals of the employee and sometimes the culture of the employer is not a good fit for the employee. Employees constantly feel frustrated with poor leadership and lack of vision of their organizations. As an employee, your perception of those issues is at the heart of why employers can't retain professionals. If you are feeling frustrated at work, these signs might be familiar to you. If so, it's time to make the break for good.

Fearlessly But Softly Resign from a Job

Your breakup has to be strategic, so I want you to put your hustler hat on and break up with your job fearlessly but softly. I think most good managers know when a resignation is coming if they are in tune with an employee's happiness. Just like when you are in a relationship with someone, you start to notice if they are not engaged, their communication starts to decrease, or they stop going above and beyond to make you happy. It's the same with jobs, but as a professional, you have to communicate more effectively with your organization about what is not going right on the job.

Before you fearlessly resign, attempt to express your concerns to leadership. If they don't make a strong attempt to improve your professional experience and exposure, then it's time to resign. Performance reviews or weekly one-on-one meetings with your manager are the best time to express your frustration, ask for more meaningful work, or explain your career goals. I like to call this a soft approach to resigning because you are not totally catching your manager off guard. The best leaders want to retain employees, and they want to know how they can improve the workplace and help their employees succeed. But bad managers usually have a revolving door in their workplace and are constantly dealing with employees breaking up with them for better job opportunities.

When we break up with jobs, we aren't just breaking up with our manager; we are also breaking up with our co-workers, clients, and HR representatives. So it's very important to value those relationships and break up softly with them as well. Follow these three best practices to make the break confidently and easily:

1. It's very important to have a pre-breakup conversation with your manager. Once you have accepted a job offer, go into their office and tell your manager that you have accepted a new job. Don't just email your resignation letter without warning.

2. If you work on a team or interface with stakeholders or clients, it's a good idea to have a pre-breakup conversation with them as well. If you were serving them or working with them on projects, you may owe them deliverables.

3. Lastly, you will have to notify your human resources department. When you break up with the HR team, this makes your resignation final. HR needs to know your last day of employment so they can process personnel paperwork and conduct an exit interview, if needed.

As you go through this career rehab journey, it's so important to do the right thing when you fearlessly resign and let your organization know in advance that you have accepted another job. You never know if you will cross paths with your manager, co-workers, clients, or HR team again. So keep your networking hat on and close out the professional relationship on a good note. Professional breakups don't have to be horrible if everyone involved conducts themselves like professionals.

Sending Out Your Breakup (Resignation) Letter

When I left my federal government job in 2014 for a senior IT consultant role at Deloitte, I was terrified. I was not worried about the new job; I was scared about resigning from my good government job. I had worked there as an IT project manager for more than five years, and now I had to break the news to my manager and team that I was leaving. I had so much anxiety about sending the resignation letter, and I'm not really sure why. Maybe it was the fear of the unknown and how I was going to handle their reaction—positive or negative. Let's be real—not every organization is going to be happy that you are leaving them for a better job. But, before I sent the resignation letter I decided to have a face-to-face conversation with leadership first because I wanted to respect our professional relationship before I caught them completely off guard. The conversation with my leadership team went very well. They were very supportive of my next move into private sector and they were actually surprised I was making such a brave decision.

So you need to understand the rules when it comes to sending out the resignation letter—or, as I call it, the breakup letter. The breakup letter is the formal way of telling your employer that you don't want to be in a relationship anymore. You need to write one even if you break up in person first; the breakup letter protects you and clearly informs everyone of your last day. To stay on everyone's good side, follow my four rules of the breakup letter:

1. Always give two weeks or more of notice when you send out your breakup letter.
2. Inform everyone of the breakup: Send your breakup letter to your leadership team, core team, and the HR office.
3. Date the letter with the breakup date (today) and your official move-out date (the last day you will be in the office).
4. Keep an official copy of your emailed breakup letter in your personal files.

Breakup letters ensure that you do the right thing by your personal brand and the company you plan to resign from.

Communication is key when you break up with your job, so always be upfront with everyone you work for so they won't feel like you are trying to hide something. When you have a staff meeting with your core team (stakeholders, customers, end users, and clients), verbally let them know you are resigning, but always send a breakup letter via email to your core leadership team. Everyone you work with does not have to receive a breakup letter, but they must be informed either in writing or in person.

When Job Breakups Go Bad

If you work long enough, you will experience a bad job breakup. This is when your organization does not take it well that you are moving on to a new role. Sometimes your manager gets mad or your co-workers are unsupportive. As you go through your career rehab journey, you will encounter professional haters. Not everyone will be happy for you when you are taking your personal brand to the next level. This can make your last two to three weeks at your old job hell, because before your move-out date arrives, you will have to transition your tasks or projects to someone else. You may feel awkward as you go through this process, but that is OK, too. When an organization or your peers treat you poorly after you resign, it's confirmation that the working relationship was never genuine anyway.

One month before I resigned from a tech company, my manager and I had a disagreement. We (the team) were under attack by another program manager and his team, and we felt we were not getting the support we needed from him. Then he accidentally sent me an email that was intended for his manager, saying things like, "Kanika thinks she is not replaceable." I was already preparing to resign, but now my manager had showed his true colors. Still, I carried out the resignation professionally. Despite how he had dealt with our disagreement, I made sure I did what was right for my personal brand. Two other employees resigned on the same day—a red flag for senior leadership. But not once did they ask to get my side of the story or try to mediate the situation. Companies will use you while they can get work out of you, and then once they don't need you or you don't need them, they turn their backs. That's why it's so important to focus on your personal brand and continue to date jobs.

And be sure to keep your resignation professional by doing the following:

→ Conduct a proper knowledge transfer with your team.
→ Communicate to your customers, clients, and stakeholders what to expect as you transition your work to the new person.
→ Effectively communicate in writing and in person the status of your project before you leave.
→ Leave the team all required documentation, artifacts, and standard operating procedures to ensure their future success.

As a solid personal brand, you should always attempt to do the right thing even when others don't. The best brands handle breakups with integrity and class. As a brand, you have to remain calm during the breakup storm. It's a good idea to think about your new career journey as you work your last two weeks. Look to your future, smile, and be grateful for the new opportunity that lies ahead.

Best Practices to Close Out Your Career Relationship

Whether the breakup process with your job goes well or badly, always close out the relationship with good intentions. Just because your manager may be mad that you are leaving does not give you the freedom to represent your brand unprofessionally. I have plenty of friends who are real estate agents, and the relationships between them and their clients don't always go well. Maybe it took a long time to find a home they really wanted to buy, or maybe it took a *very* long time to sell a homeowner's home. But the agent must remain professional even after they go to closing. It's the same with your career breakups. You have to close out the relationship while staying professional at all times.

Below I have listed three ways you can close out a fearless resignation and ensure that your personal brand stays intact and integrity-focused after you depart from an organization.

1. Send a goodbye email to everyone. In writing, go out of your way to show your appreciation and gratitude to your manager, co-workers, and clients. Let them know how this position has added value to your career expertise and personal brand.

2. Provide your professional contact information just in case they need to ask you something about a task or project or just to stay in touch. Remember, these contacts are now a part of your network, and they can always be a resource to you or you can be a resource to them.

3. On your last day, go out of your way to say goodbye to those who meant the most to you. It's a great way to show your appreciation in person and to extend your gratitude.

Fearless resignations don't mean you have to be abrasive or rude about breaking up with a job. The fearless approach is all about taking control of your career happiness. The lack of resignation hesitation keeps your focus on moving forward. So often we let the idea of resigning hold us back from doing what we should have years ago. Over time, breaking up with jobs becomes a lot easier, and it will free you of those career burdens.

☆ Meet Armand Hodge, Corporate Rebel

My client Armand Hodge dated several jobs before he landed an awesome opportunity at Boeing. Armand always had a passion for marketing and communications, but he wanted to mash it up with tech. I started coaching Armand when he was a consultant working as a federal government contractor, but he was unhappy in that role. He shared with me that he wanted to work for a Fortune 500 company on projects that involved digital transformation, product management, and digital marketing. Armand is one of my corporate rebel clients. He had been in industry for more than five years, but he was having a hard time finding a company that aligned with his dreams and career goals. He developed a fearless mindset and has mastered the art of breaking up with jobs.

☆ *Introduce yourself, your company, and your career expertise.*

☆ My name is Armand Hodge. I currently work at Boeing as a technology communications and branding specialist. #TechIsMyGrind and #CommsIsMyWildRabbit. My career expertise focuses on the convergence of communications and technology—how the two industries help each other.

Armand Hodge, continued

⭐ *Since being in career rehab with me as your career coach, how has resigning from jobs become easier?*

⭐ It honestly feels like second nature. Being in career rehab with you gave me that extra push that I needed to jump off the cliff and move to the next level in my career. In the past, I would feel a sense of guilt when it came to resigning from jobs. Once I started my journey with career rehab, I realized that I owed it to myself to be happy in my desired career field.

⭐ *When you resigned from your last role and took a new job with Boeing, did you feel like all your new company offerings and incentives were worth the resignation?*

⭐ Absolutely! It was honestly one of the best decisions I made in my life. Taking my new job at Boeing was a breath of fresh air. If you've ever seen the miniseries *The Jacksons: An American Dream,* remember the part when Berry Gordy told Michael that if he performed at Motown's 25th anniversary special that it would knock him into the stratosphere? I feel like transitioning into tech and taking my new job with Boeing really knocked me into the stratosphere.

⭐ *What new benefits are you getting out of your new role that make you happy about the direction of your career?*

⭐ I'm able to learn more about my industry and gain new technical skills to become well-versed in tech. I'm able to take advantage of phenomenal professional development opportunities. There are also plenty of opportunities for me to connect and receive mentorship from some great leaders within the company. I've always wanted to gain knowledge within and outside my industry on an international level. It's truly amazing to work with teammates in multiple states and countries across the globe.

⭐ *Any advice to professionals who are scared to resign from a role that they are currently miserable in or not growing in?*

⭐ Follow your gut! Walk through the door and go after your goals. If you have that feeling that there is something out there for you much bigger than this, it's time for you to leave! You owe it to yourself to be happy in your career field. Don't let fear hold

Armand Hodge, continued

you back. Look at it like this: You control your own happiness. The only way you will get happy within your career is if YOU first leave a bad situation. Once you leave that situation of feeling like you're in the sunken place, the opportunities and blessings will start flowing in.

☆ ☆ ☆

DON'T OVERCOMMIT TO WORK

As you take on new roles, it's important to start the new career relationship the way you want it to be for as long as you plan to date that job. Don't overcommit too early in the relationship until you have decided how you want the career relationship to be maintained. As you date jobs, it's important to pay attention to early signs of corporate dysfunction, including imbalanced leadership styles, strained teamwork dynamics, lack of training resources, lack of diversity, and overworked teams. But sometimes our anxiety and excitement overpower our logic and we don't see the dynamics clearly in the first three to six months.

We all want to do a great job when we land a new role, but keep in mind how to balance your personal life and work life as you attempt to do it all. Trying to be superwoman or superman early in the job relationship will only lead to quick burnout. In this chapter, you will learn to manage career burnout by setting boundaries with your employer and not allowing them to overwork you on a regular basis. You will also learn how to start a career relationship with a new job so they will fully understand your position on maintaining a healthy work-life balance. Finally, you will learn how to use tools and technology to help you work more efficiently.

Set the Career Relationship Pace

You are in the driver's seat, so don't be afraid to set your work pace in the first 90 days. Just like when you date someone, you learn a lot about your new employer in the first three to four months. During this stage, you should be evaluating what you like and dislike about them as you get to learn the people, the culture, and your responsibilities.

The first 90 days is your career relationship trial period, and it may look something like this:

→ *First 30 days.* When you start a new role, it's important to really observe the culture of your new organization. Analyze when people come to work and when they leave to go home. This will tell you a lot about how to set your work schedule and whether your team values working from home and flexible work schedules.

→ *First 60 days.* Clearly understand the expectations of your role. Ask your management team and co-workers what you should expect from your daily tasks and regular meetings. Also try to shadow your teammates and management team before you are fully thrown to the wolves on a specific project.

→ *First 90 days.* At this point you should be able to identify the subject matter experts on your team. These will be the go-to folks who can help when you are stuck on a deliverable or don't understand an organization policy or office politics. Make sure you are creating a strong circle of trust so you can easily navigate work-related challenges.

How to Start a New Career Relationship

It's essential for organizations to clearly explain what they want you to do when you start a new job. But it's also your responsibility to ask within the first couple of weeks. Many professionals start new roles without really knowing how much time they will need to devote to a particular task or how flexible their work schedule can be if they would like to work from home. To set the expectations and boundaries for your work-life balance, address the following four issues with your direct supervisor:

1. Clearly communicate your work schedule.
2. Find out the actual percentage of time you will be spending on specific tasks or projects.
3. Ask if you will be able to work from home a few times per week.
4. Find out how your manager and supervisor will be rating your performance.

Don't make the mistake of not addressing these issues early on, because once you have created bad working habits, you may start to think a good work-life balance doesn't exist. But there are always ways to stay healthy as you attempt to juggle your personal life and your work life.

Balance Work and Life

The concept of work-life balance is simply creating a boundary between your job and your personal life. This boundary line is your responsibility to set, because if you wait for your organization to do it, it may never get done. Cool geeks have an opportunity to set these boundaries now for the rest of your life, so make sure to set them when you start working your first real job. For corporate rebels, it's not too late for you to set boundaries—it just requires a mindset shift. And for those career dropouts who have retired, enjoy your freedom! And maybe offer some advice from time to time for the rest of us, who are working toward that goal ourselves.

The real question is: Do we tip the balance toward life or work? Or do we attempt to balance both equally? There are only 24 hours in a day, and it's simply impossible to accomplish everything. That's why there is always tomorrow. It's OK to carry over things from one day into the next.

I admit I have yet to master the concept of work-life balance. I have struggled with it for years, reading books that taught me new tricks to being wife, daughter, sister, business owner, career coach, and IT professional, all at the same time. Even celebrities and politicians strain to manage their lives, despite the glamour we see on TV.

When I think about Michelle Obama, whom I admire so much, I always wonder how she manages her career, marriage, and motherhood. I know when she was in the White House, she had more help from her staff, but before she became first lady, I can only imagine the stress she must have encountered as a working mom.

One thing I have conquered is not overdosing on a job. In my 20s, I had way more energy to work late and at night if I had a deliverable. I was eager to please management and outwork my team members. I was always trying to prove that I was better than everyone else, but it was costing me sleep, health, and time with family. I was working so hard that I was missing out on key events and celebrations in my family. Not to mention that at this point in my career I was not making a very high salary, but I had brainwashed myself to believe that the harder I worked, the more reward I would get. That is true in most cases, but the extra hours per day don't mean you will always be promoted or recognized for your hard work. Your quality of work is the important thing. How you get to the finish line should never really matter to leadership.

I now believe in working a hard eight hours and taking your butt home. The idea of coming into the office early and staying late and still not accomplishing much during that time explains a lot about many workers. We as career rehabbers have to learn how to work smarter, not harder. As you grow in your career rehab journey, you will learn how to think strategically about your plan to execute your workload. Try these tips to help you work smarter, not harder:

→ Always set your personal deadline for your deliverables before the actual due date. This gives you time to make revisions if you have to conduct peer reviews with others.

→ Work on your most important tasks on the days you have a lighter workload or fewer meetings to attend.

→ Attempt to complete your important tasks before others get into the office; this will eliminate distractions and conversations.

→ Leverage your relationships with your co-workers: Find out if there is a template or standard operating procedure (SOP) you can follow so you don't have to reinvent the wheel for your work.

Work Faster with Technology

In this digital age, professionals should be able to adopt new tools and technologies to get their work done faster. This career rehab journey is all about becoming more efficient in producing quality deliverables so you can build your personal career brand. Being able to try new tools and assessing what works just requires an open mind. For so long, you may have been working the same job or doing the same task, and you may have been doing it the long way. An open-minded approach to a production audit will increase your productivity and decrease feelings of stress and anxiety. Professionals spend a lot of time tracking conversations and information through email and manually keeping track of their calendars, which is a pain in the ass. Projects are suffering because teams are not effectively collaborating or communicating ongoing changes. Organizations are working in silos, which is frustrating professionals who are forced to stay late every day. Productivity starts with organization. If you fail to be organized, you will not succeed.

Productivity Technology Tools

I have been in the IT industry for 15 years, and I have found these five tools very valuable to my professional success:

1. *Calendly.* This is a super easy tool that allows you to automatically schedule meetings and appointments for your online calendar. This tool sends a notification to your email and places the scheduled meeting on your calendar and the requestor's calendar.

2. *Jira.* A project management tool that teams use to gather project requirements and assign user stories and tasks to team members. It also tracks progress, assigns due dates, and allows you to attach documents.

3. *Slack.* An online tool that teams can use to communicate and collaborate on projects. This tool cuts down on emails because you can use the app to talk to the entire group or to individuals. No more chasing down emails!

4. *Google Drive.* This free product allows me to create documents and save them in the cloud, which is linked to my free Gmail email account. Google Drive is a great way to back up your computer files and share them with other contributors.

5. *Zoom.* A free online conferencing tool that allows you to conduct video meetings, record webinars, and host team meetings. You can use this tool to share your screen with the attendees and allow them to share their computer screen with you.

As the workforce continues to evolve, productivity tools and applications will continue to enhance our quality of work and speed of delivery. These innovative tools were created to help us manage our workload and decrease our stress, anxiety, and depression. Your personal brand will evolve at a much faster rate if you adopt a few of these tools as you manage your life and career.

Put Yourself First

You will spend on average more than 90,000 hours of your life at work, according to a 2018 article in *Business Insider*. (This number does not include overtime.) When do professionals have time for their personal lives? Growing up, I watched my parents work overtime and weekends for their entire career, which was more than 32 years of my life. They were both considered "essential professionals," who had to report to work even during snowstorms. My mother and I often chat about her career and the sacrifices she made. Now in retirement, she has more time to herself and can reflect on everything she missed out on while she was working. It's important to make time for yourself now, while you are still working. Your personal life, family, and health matter now. Don't wait until you retire to focus on the things that matter today.

Your organization clearly knows what they expect of you for eight hours a day. What do you expect from yourself while you are at work? As a professional on this career rehab journey, it is important to build your brand dating these jobs, but to have a healthy relationship with your job you first have to have a healthy relationship with yourself. So make a conscious decision to put your wants and needs before the job. I have made the mistake of working extremely hard and not saving anything for myself. Below I have identified simple actions that will help you love yourself throughout the workday. Here are ten ways to focus on YOU:

1. *Pray or meditate daily.* It helps you ease your mind before your day begins and promotes positivity in your life.
2. *Work a hard eight hours and go home.* Working longer hours may only mean something to you. Once you have done all you can do in those eight hours, leave on time.
3. *Turn your work mobile phone off once you have finished work.* There is no need to respond to every call or email that

CAREER REHAB

comes through after work hours. You can follow up with them the next business day.

4. *Work out three to five times a week for one hour.* It will help you feel and look better, as well as help you cope with work-related stress. It's so important to take care of your cardiovascular health.

5. *Eat healthy meals* throughout the day to stay energized and keep yourself looking great.

6. *Take daily walks while at work*; a change of scenery will help you feel better. It's not a good thing to spend your entire day in your office. Get outside and get a good dose of Vitamin D.

7. *Make time for routine doctor appointments.* So often we work so hard that we neglect our health. When you are not feeling well, follow up with your doctor and get diagnosed early.

8. *Schedule monthly massages for your body.* For those who sit at computers daily and those who have labor-intensive jobs, deep tissue massages help ease the pain in your upper and lower back.

9. *Sign up for non-work-related classes or online courses that interest you.* This will help you learn new topics and skills outside your job duties.

10. *Embrace your hobbies, talents, and gifts outside work.* Too often we focus on our career-related skills and neglect our other abilities. Your hobbies and passions will help keep you sane.

YOU Are the Balance

Some days you will have your work-life balance all together, and some days you won't. But that's OK! You are not a failure because your life and job are not 100 percent on track. You can still do small things to keep your life manageable even when things are going wrong. Life happens, and unforeseen events like death, car accidents, health problems, and financial issues may shake up your world. But you can't fix everything at once. You have to take things one at a time. Go for the small wins some days, and on days when you have more time or flexibility go for the big wins. Either way, you are winning because some progress is better than none. I think we overcomplicate the idea of getting things done, which then leads to stress, anxiety, and depression. We all know you can't get anything done being SAD (stressed, anxious, and depressed).

Often we give too much power to our to-do list. The to-do list has become a tool of evil. We look at it and only get more discouraged. I try to finish just a few items per day. It's a good idea to break out your to-do list into small chunks of work. It looks more manageable, and it's more easily achievable.

☆ Meet Shamira Redd, Corporate Rebel Who Took Her Career Control Back

Shamira Redd earned her BS in accounting from Pennsylvania State University in 2014 and obtained her tax certification in 2015. She then received her MBA from the University of Maryland University College. A self-described overachiever, she worked a full-time job as an accountant at a private law firm in Washington, DC, while pursuing her MBA. Then she reclaimed control of her career.

Can you explain a time when you overdosed on work and how it led to a burnout? Did you experience stress, anxiety, and depression?

I was working to the extreme, and extreme meaning arriving at 6 A.M. and leaving a little past midnight. I am the person who works and puts her all in it. I really enjoy being an overachiever and giving 110 percent, and most of all, I like what I do. It seems there is always some suspense and challenge being an accountant. Being young and soaking up all the knowledge from my peers has also helped me become more structured and create a meaningful lifestyle.

Needless to say, while doing all of the above I was burnt out and went through a very crucial time at my job while attending my master's program. My new position led me to a new supervisor. We did not see eye to eye. I don't quite remember when the animosity began. Not too long after I accepted the position, my peer received a supervisor title. From looking inside out, it was obvious that she was in need of

Shamira Redd, continued

management training. Perhaps it all began shortly after I mentioned that I was obtaining my master's and my schedule needed to change, which was slight and viable as a salaried employee. Nonetheless, my work ethic never changed, but it seems she started assigning her duties to me. So, yes, I was in my humble skin and never spoke up and just did as I was instructed. I was doing my best to stay focused on the job as a whole and not let a bad seed interfere with my soul, but honestly it was hard, especially working directly with the person.

At this point, it was an everyday battle. She created a hostile work environment for me. It went from the overload on work to the vulgar emails I was receiving on a daily basis. We were in and out of the human resources department. I felt like I was sinking and swimming at the same time trying to balance it all out. My assignments were becoming more advanced as I excelled further into my program, and I was so overwhelmed and stressed beyond measure. My body changed tremendously. My blood pressure was high for the first time ever in my adult life, and I was losing my appetite but somehow becoming overweight for my age. I had developed a nerve disease called Raynaud's disease; the number one cause of this disease is stress. My doctor hinted to me that whatever it is, I needed to let it go. It was shortly after my trip to Africa and upon my return that I realized I had to leave my job. A few months later, after ensuring my financials were in place in order to take the leap, and speaking with a few people including you, I prayed and left my job. It was not something I wanted to do, but I had to be honest with myself and stand firm with my decision. Thereafter, I focused solely on completing my master's while getting myself together.

☆ *What have you learned from overdosing on work? How do you better manage your relationship with your current job?*

☆ I have learned to take my health more seriously and, more importantly, myself. Love thyself first! My health includes the mental, physical, emotional, and spiritual well-being. I learned that I was replaceable, so if I dropped dead, the position will be posted within 24 hours—guaranteed. My situation has taught me a lot, and I am now able to say thank you for the process. It was necessary! I am better!

I better manage my relationship with my current job by demonstrating open communication. Also, I establish boundaries and understand the expectations and

Shamira Redd, continued

need of the position, so we can further accomplish the goal. I like to reciprocate what is expected of the manager to the manager, which in turn builds a two-way relationship. I also continue to be valuable, whether I am working independently or on a team, by bringing my best in all that I do.

Q *What productivity tools or technologies do you use to manage your life and deliverables at work?*

A The best productivity tools are staying current on software. Every company uses different software that spits out similar information, and for that reason, taking the time to go over tutorials and familiarizing myself with the software is important to me. Another productivity tool which is key is time management. We work many hours. I am old school mixed with new school and a firm believer in writing it out. I have a planner that is in full use. I also have a second helper, which is the technology piece that helps me balance, an app called Evernote and Microsoft OneNote, which allows me to better manage my life.

Q *How do you focus on yourself? Identify your personal goals, hobbies, and professional goals.*

A Self-care is very important to me. It can be something as simple as attending to my basic needs and being gentle with myself. The basic needs include my mental, physical, emotional, and spiritual well-being. I now acknowledge my pain and take full responsibility for my feelings. This comes after asking the question to myself on several occasions, *Am I loving myself or am I abandoning myself?* I ensure that I feed my mind daily with fruits of positivity and faith.

I enjoy yoga, reading, horseback riding, nature, spa dates, traveling, puzzles, and volunteering. Personal goals of mine include being a better me at all costs, becoming debt free, and enjoying my choice of direction in life. I am all about setting small goals in order to achieve the larger ones, which creates opportunities to challenge myself more often. My professional goals are widespread because my accounting and business career can relate to many different things. Currently, I would like to obtain my CPA, be proficient in developing productive relationships, and venture into the consulting field.

13

☆ ☆ ☆

COMMUTES WORTH THE COINS

As you work to design your ideal career, it's perfectly fine if you don't want a long commute. Remember that you create the balance between your personal life and your work life. I think most professionals have had at least one job that was more than an hour away from their home. If this doesn't apply to you, that's awesome! But if you're like me, you may have had to travel 90 minutes each way to and from work at some point. As I look back at that time, some of these sacrifices changed my life and made me a better professional. After I graduated from college, I was offered a full-time job at Verizon, but I lived an hour away, and the only way to get there on time was to leave the house at 6 A.M.; any later, and the commute would take me two hours rather than one. At this point, I was only making $55,000 per year, but I was still living at home with my parents, so I thought I was rich. So technically, the commute was worth the coins because I was only responsible for paying my car loan and cell phone bill. I was saving most of my pay to buy a condo. My career blueprint was not yet designed, and I was just happy to be working for a big company like Verizon. But over time, the drive became a pain in the ass. With the hour in the morning and 90 minutes at night, I was spending far too much time on the road. I started to feel unhappy every day.

According to 2016 U.S. Census Bureau data, most workers have an average one-way drive time of about 26.1 minutes in the U.S.; per a 2013 Census Bureau study, nearly 600,000 Americans drive "mega commutes" of at least 90 minutes and 50 or more miles. Professionals with long commutes may experience unhappiness, higher blood pressure, and headaches. Some employees feel like they are missing out on leisure activities like attending happy hours, going to the gym, and cooking dinner every night.

Many professionals take the first job offer they get because they have a sense of urgency after being unemployed for some time. The pressure of having to provide for their families makes them feel like a job with a long commute is the best they can do. But that's why you need a job search strategy based around where you currently live, if you want to stay sane and happy. In this chapter, you will learn how to put yourself first, despite the demands of raising a family and dealing with a long commute to a job that may not be paying you very well. You will also learn how to find a job closer to home and how to search for remote jobs.

Find Jobs Near Home

It's easy to believe that shorter commutes are linked to happiness. I can imagine most employees skipping to work if their commute were less than 30 minutes from their home. They could get to the gym every day after work and still enjoy dinner with their families. Working closer to home also makes life much easier on working parents, who can more easily get to the day care or school in an emergency or if their child is sick. Professionals can even go home for lunch if they work really close to home. Career rehab is all about restoring what you think the job has stolen from you—perhaps that's time. Jobs are robbing professionals of reasonable commutes and not allowing them to work from home. But it's up to you to push the reset button on your commute and find jobs closer to home.

According to a 2017 article in *Business Insider*, adding 20 minutes to your commute each day has the same negative effect on your job satisfaction as a 19 percent pay cut would.

If you want to work closer to home, stick to the shorter commute job search rules. If you become too flexible with your commuting options, you will fall right back into a longer commute. Keep this formula in mind as you consider your ideal commute:

Shorter Work Commute + Job Satisfaction = Career Happiness

Then, put a strategy in place for your commute plan:

→ Identify a range of miles you are willing to travel from home. For example, say you are willing to travel 20 miles or less from your ZIP code, so you can be at work in less than one hour.

→ When recruiters call or email you, decline any interviews in locations that don't fall inside your designated commute zone. Inform them where you are willing to work so they can update your information in their system. Remember, the recruiters are your career agents, so work with the ones who specialize in placing people in the areas you're interested in.

→ Create a job alert on the job board websites so you can get automatic notifications of new job postings in your chosen area.

→ Apply to jobs close to your home and follow up with recruiters who have identified roles they can help you get close to your home.

High-Paying Remote Jobs

The closer you live to a major city, the higher the cost of living. When you live further out, the cost of your home is usually cheaper. But when professionals work farther away from their homes, the commute can become a nightmare. Taking public transportation to work eases the pain, but what if you could work from home full time or part time? Would that make you happier? Currently, I work from home two days a week and it really eases my stress levels. As someone who is not a fan of public transportation, I look forward to working from my laptop every Tuesday and Friday. I worked from home five days a week for a couple of years, making six figures as a mobile UX architect, and I loved every moment. But in 2019, I took a new role in Washington, DC, near the White House, and it takes me an hour to get to work. The commute is manageable with the two telework days (and it allows me more time to work with my career coaching clients). When I started the job, I was commuting five days a week with no telework options, and it was killing me. I would cry to my husband, saying, "I can't do this. I am so exhausted." I truly miss working remotely five days a week, but I like the people I work with, so it makes those days in the office worth the drive.

Over the past few years, terms like *work from home, telecommute, virtual,* and *remote* have become very popular in online job postings. As I researched finding a remote job, I developed a formula for myself and my career coaching clients.

Identify Careers That Support Remote Work

The key to finding a high-paying remote position is identifying which job titles and cutting-edge skills you need to work remotely. Professions like IT, engineering, health care, customer service, project management, and recruiting can often be done remotely. But keep in mind that most high-paying remote jobs also require you to know how to use webinar technologies, online database systems, and document repositories.

Leverage Remote Job Search Keywords

As I searched for remote jobs, I discovered many companies use different terms to describe them. I began to use all the following terms in my searches: *remote, work from home, virtual, telecommute,* and *partial remote.* When you search by these keywords individually, you'll find all types of positions that may fall under the remote work umbrella.

Once you identify the right keywords, it's time to pair them with the relevant jobs. In my search, I wanted to narrow my results to roles like project manager, product manager, senior consultant, and product owner, so I tried variations like "remote project manager," "telecommute senior consultant," and "work from home product manager." I also paired these keywords with relevant skills, like "remote agile," "telecommute WordPress," and "work from home SharePoint."

Leave Out Location Constraints

By default, most job sites use your location to narrow down the available jobs by your city, state, and/or ZIP code. But when you search for remote jobs, you should double-check to make sure this field is either blank or changed to "Remote." This will widen your search criteria and give you more relevant results. After all, most companies won't require you to live in the same state or country as the company headquarters.

Create Remote Job Alerts

Most popular job sites, including Glassdoor, allow you to create job alerts, which notify you of new job openings based on a specific job title, salary, or location. These alerts might come in the form of a daily or weekly email or a mobile app notification. When I was actively looking for a remote job, I created an alert for each remote keyword listed earlier and each job title I was interested in—for example, "remote project manager," "telecommute agile," "work from home," etc.

Find Out Which Companies Hire Remote Workers

Thousands of companies hire large numbers of remote workers. Amazon, Dell, GitHub, IBM, and Humana are just a few of the many private-sector companies that offer remote information technology, health care, or customer service opportunities. In my search, I discovered, applied to, and interviewed with companies I had never heard of before. The appeal of working from home helped me stay open-minded to small and large organizations.

The key to career happiness is finding what works for you. Personally, I found I'm happy working in my pajamas and having the freedom to get things done at home for my family. It may take a while, but don't give up on finding a remote position. If you dedicate a couple of hours a day to searching for and applying to opportunities, you might be enjoying your new remote job in no time.

☆ Meet Monica Newman, Corporate Rebel and Smart Commuter

Monica Newman is the program coordinator for Our Place Waldorf, a nonprofit organization that provides meals to the homeless population. As a corporate rebel, Monica is invested in her career and has made the commuting moves necessary to help her retain job satisfaction.

Q: *Explain what your commute was like when you first started working with me. Describe your commuting obstacles.*

A: My daily commute was 2.5 to 3 hours, and that's when I drove to work. Depending on the day and what Waze said, I took the train. My commute started at the beginning of the green line and took me to the end of the red line. On those days, my commute was about 2 hours and 30 minutes. Once I began driving, my commute was approximately 3 hours and 25 minutes. I lived in Waldorf, Maryland, and worked in Rockville, Maryland, so I hit all three major areas of traffic: Route 5, 495, and I-270. At first, I thought it would be cool taking the train and grabbing coffee on the way in. That looks good on *Sex and the City*, but it wasn't for me. This was my commute, and I did not factor in dropping the kids off at school.

Monica Newman, continued

Q *How did your old work commute affect personal life, family life, work-life balance, etc.?*

A My commute started to ruin my life and affect my mental health, although I really liked my job and the people I worked with. In the beginning it was tolerable, but I couldn't deal with getting home at 6:30 or 7:00 P.M. sometimes. I have a family, and my tiredness started to throw everything off . . . it turned into me forgetting to do things for them and myself. I felt way too stressed out. I had no more balance; it was my job or my happiness. My job became more like an escape from my home life; I only really loved my job because I got away. That wasn't normal at all. I was the cause of my lack of help at home, and my commute was to blame. My mental health was really taking a toll, and I had to speak to someone about how I was feeling. Some days were good, and others not so much. On good days when traffic wasn't backed up and my drive was maybe an hour, I could bump Drake and clear my mind. Nonetheless, a change had to be made, and stepping out on faith was the best thing I ever did, so I searched for a career coach and found you. You really inspired me, seeing another woman bettering herself and taking control of her career and life. You motivated me to do the same. I knew I wanted to become this very successful woman. I just didn't know how or where to start.

Q *Are you happier now that you have a better work commute? Do you work from home some days?*

A My life has turned around in a much more positive way. I'm happier and more creative than before. I say that because I have time for things I thought about doing back when I was sitting in traffic. Now I work from home two days a week.

Q *What advice would you give a mother, wife, or single woman who is scared to leave their current role for a new job?*

A I would advise anyone to really think about what they want and write out job goals along with personal ones. Once you have everything lined up for a job, God will make a way for your new one. It's really all about having faith in yourself. Sacrifices have to be made to become who you want to be.

Prior to becoming a career mom, I was in the Navy for eight years with just one child at the time. Once I was honorably discharged, I enrolled in school and got my degree

Monica Newman, continued

as a medical assistant. My resume wasn't the best. I had lots of valuable skills. I just didn't know having a better resume or someone to assist me would make a world of difference. I spoke with you and we revamped my resume, and within the first two months, I had four interviews and three job offers, two of which were with the federal government. I never imagined me, a single mother with two kids, negotiating my own salary with the government. I knew if that was possible, what more could I achieve? I was offered a position at the Naval Research Lab (38 minutes from home). At my interview, I explained how ideal this position would be for me, along with knowing I could go back to school and continue my degree. Two weeks after being offered the position, I had another interview that I wasn't going to take, but I did. It was for a position at a nonprofit organization (five minutes from my house). I work three days a week from our soup kitchen and two days from home.

☆ ☆ ☆

LIFE AFTER
RETIREMENT

According to a 2014 Gallup poll, the average retirement age in the U.S. has increased to 62. Many workers are putting off retirement because their savings and investment accounts have taken a hit. I like to call my career coaching clients who plan to retire soon career dropouts, because they are dropping their working life for life in retirement. Retirement is what all professionals are working toward. In some people's minds, that is when they will finally have the freedom to do what they want. The thought of being told what to do at a job for more than 35 years sounds painful, but retirement can be similar to the feeling when a homeowner pays off his or her home: They feel a huge sense of financial freedom from having to make that monthly mortgage payment. Professionals who retire get a chance to experience career freedom. The Baby Boomers, who are reaching retirement age now were some of the most loyal to their employers. I watched my Boomer mother give more than 35 years of her life to the Washington, DC, government.

That's why career rehab isn't just for college graduates and working professionals; it's also for retirees, because they have all the time in the world to reinvent themselves as they travel, volunteer, or start a new career or business. Many retirees don't have to worry about long commutes, raising children, or working late. They can focus on what will make them happy. My mom retired a few years ago, and since she left her government job, we often chat about her work life compared to her retirement life. We also talk about getting ready for retirement; as professionals get close to retiring, it's important to prepare physically, mentally, and financially. In this chapter, you will learn how to properly prepare for retirement by saving more money and diversifying your investments into stocks, IRAs, and 401(k) retirement plans. You will also learn how to change your mindset for retirement and decide how you would like to spend your free time or find a new job, either in working part time or consulting.

Prepare for Life After Retirement

Since the average retirement age in the U.S. is 62, your career can start to feel like a 30-year mortgage, especially if you have worked at the same company or organization for most of that time. The beginning of the retirement journey could feel uncertain for some professionals who don't really know what they plan to do when they leave the work force. If your children are all grown and moved out and now your work is finished, what's left? You have given more than 30 years of your life to a career that helped you pay off a house, put your children through college, and enjoy a decent living, according to the typical definition of the "American Dream."

Most professionals have a general idea of when they plan to retire, but do they know how to prepare for it? Or do they wait until the last minute to activate their retirement planning? As you enter into this new stage of your personal journey, you want to feel good about your money, health, and family stability. Let's look at five ways you can prepare to transition from your career into retirement:

1. Research a health-care plan that will work well for you. As we get older, we need to ensure our health care covers what we need while remaining affordable. It's not a good idea to assume Medicare will provide the coverage you will need in your retirement.

2. Communicate your retirement date to your spouse. You may choose to retire at different times, or you may plan to retire together. It's vital to communicate with each other if you plan to retire before your spouse so your living expenses are covered.

3. Assess your financials: retirement income, 401(k) plan, Social Security benefits, investments, and current living expenses. After retirement, you may have to live off an adjusted income, so it's important to eliminate debt, pay off your home, and properly protect your outside investments: stocks, Roth and traditional IRAs, bonds, etc.

4. Identify some passions and interests you would like to pursue once you retire. Retirement equals freedom—it's your time to do all the things you never had time to do while working. Make a list: If you want to take classes, start a new business, or volunteer for a cause, now's the time to do it.

5. Work in advance with your HR department to properly execute your retirement exit strategy. Your HR specialist or representative is like your mortgage broker: They should be able to guide you through the retirement process. HR will help you gather and submit all your personnel documentation and ensure that you will receive your retirement benefits.

Eight Retirement Planning Tools and Calculators

If you are getting ready to retire soon, you need some tools to help you properly plan and project your retirement financials.

Financial technology company SmartAsset recommends the following eight retirement planning software tools:

1. Personal Capital
2. Quicken
3. Intuit Mint
4. WealthTrace
5. MoneyGuidePro
6. Moneytree
7. Advizr
8. RightCapital

Try some of these out (many offer a free trial period or free app functions) to see what works best for you.

Prepare for Unstable Social Security Benefits

Since I was old enough to work, I have heard my parents say Social Security will no longer be around when I retire. I am projected to retire in 2040, and the thought of paying into Social Security every two weeks just to find out the money will not be around for me to collect is discouraging. In 2019, the AARP reported that Social Security and related retirement benefits will be depleted by 2035, meaning that "the system will exhaust its cash reserves and will be able to pay out only what it takes in year-to-year in Social Security taxes."

As a career rehabber, you should always prepare for the worst. Remember that your personal brand can survive into retirement. So what are you paying into Social Security, and what qualifies you for this possible retirement benefit? According to the AARP, to qualify for retirement benefits you must have 40 Social Security credits, which you can earn by paying Social Security taxes on your income; you can earn up to four credits per calendar year. In 2019, $1,360 of income equaled one credit.

If you want an idea of your possible Social Security retirement benefits, you can use a retirement estimator. But career rehab means "keeping it real," so you must diversify your benefits without including Social Security in your planning, just in case it is no longer offered by 2035. Remember: The government does not govern your career happiness and freedom. You are in control. When you get paid in money, power, and respect, you will learn to value your retirement investments early. Career rehabbers rely on themselves to make things happen in their lives.

Five Ways to Land a New Job in Retirement

Part-time, consulting, seasonal, or freelance work are the most popular types of jobs among retirees, because they can maintain their freedom as they collect their retirement benefits. The awesome thing about landing a new job in retirement is that you can always dump it if you are financially comfortable with your retirement investments.

Below I have outlined five ways you can land a new job as a retiree:

1. Update your resume, especially if you have been working at the same organization for a while.
2. Align your resume with the types of roles you plan on taking. Make a strong attempt to update your professional experience with the correct keywords and technologies most companies are looking for.
3. Brush up on your technical skills. Make sure you know how to use computerized systems, smartphones, and tablets, since most jobs will require you to use at least one of these. You can enhance your skills by taking courses at a community college or online at elearning websites like Udemy, Coursera, or YouTube.
4. If you want a part-time job, short-term role, or consulting gig, network with your old contacts or reconnect with organizations you used to work for to see if they are hiring. You can

reuse your institutional knowledge and expertise at your old organization or at one that does similar work.

5. Upload your updated resume on Indeed and LinkedIn to begin applying to jobs in your area. As you search for jobs, use the following keywords: part time, short term, temporary, and consultant.

Best Jobs for Retirees

They say 70 is the new 40—and there's some truth to that. Retirees are more active than ever, and there is a world of exciting and fulfilling career options available to them. Most of the jobs listed below can be part time or seasonal roles at companies and organizations within your community. If you are looking to land a job just to have something to do, these roles are a great fit for you:

→ Retail cashier
→ Caretaker
→ Housesitter
→ Uber/Lyft driver
→ School bus driver
→ Substitute teacher
→ Administrative clerk
→ Hotel concierge
→ Pet sitter
→ Tax preparer

No matter what you decide to do during retirement, make sure being healthy and happy is at the top of the list. As you get older, you should really be focusing more on personal happiness. Career happiness is nothing without personal happiness. Personal happiness is an evolution, of course, and during your career rehab retirement journey, your life will evolve because you have total control over your career. You have time to be your very best as you get older.

☆ Meet Kelly Harris,
Career Dropout (and My Mother!)

Kelly Harris is my mother. She was raised and educated in Washington, DC, and spent more than 35 years working for the District of Columbia government. In 2013, she retired from her job as an inspector for the Department of Public Works and embarked on the next phase of her career: retirement.

Q: How long have you been retired? What have you learned most about yourself since you retired?

A: I retired a few years ago. I have learned to cherish the simple moments in life. I value my health more, my family more and my time. When we are working, we don't always have enough time to value the simple things in life. Also, I have learned to give more of myself to others now that I have more time to spare. It's important to be there for family during times of illness, death, and personal hardship. We can replace a car, house, or clothes, but we can't replace our good times with our families. Time and people are things we can't get back. Once time slips away and loved ones die, all we will have is the good or bad memories. Retirement life has taught me to live my life with no regrets.

Q: When you were working, did you feel like you were professionally miserable, or did you love your career? Any advice to the younger work force as they plan their careers?

A: If it's something you have a whole lot of interest in and enjoy doing, it will not seem like work. It's so important to pursue a career that will bring career happiness. I spent most of my career working jobs I was not overly crazy about. I always told my two daughters and other young people to get educated, study for professional certifications, and work various roles so they can build their professional skills and remain marketable.

Q: What should professionals do financially, physically, and mentally to help them prepare for retirement?

A: During your retirement life, it's very important to feel whole as much as you can, because you have given up so much while you were working. So proper preparation

Kelly Harris, continued

and planning is vital as you begin to think about your retirement date. Retirement life is a trade-off because you will be making less money per month and you will be getting older. Here are my tips for making it work:

→ *Financially*. You should save and invest as much money as you can. It's so important to diversify your investments and pay off your home.

→ *Physically*. Have an exercise program that you enjoy in place. Also make sure you eat foods that control obesity and heal any of your health issues.

→ *Mentally*. I recommend doing a lot of soul searching by thinking about the things you will enjoy doing that you didn't have time for and wanted to do while working. Also spend some time praying and meditating on your hobbies, passion, and purpose in life.

Overall, as you prepare for retirement, you want peace of mind. You don't want to worry about things you could have prepared for while you were working.

How do you like to spend your time now in retirement? What activities are you looking forward to doing in retirement?

I like doing all the things that I didn't have time to do while working. I enjoy walking five to six times a week. That is also my prayer and meditation time to talk to the Lord, thanking him for all the blessings he has given me and my family. I enjoy having time to notice the beauty of all the things God has made. I'm looking forward to becoming closer to God and enjoying a good line dance class. Also I am looking forward to helping my family when they need me. I am also looking forward to traveling and seeing new destinations within the United States and outside of the United States. I plan to always keep my passport ready so me and my husband can travel and see the world during my awesome and peaceful journey I'm on right now.

☆ ☆ ☆

DIVORCE THE JOB FOR THE DREAM

I have always wanted to own and run a successful business. In 2013, I started to seriously pursue entrepreneurship while I was still working for the federal government. But it felt more like I was cheating on my job with my business as a speaker, author, and career coach. I self-published a successful book called *Life Rehab: Don't Overdose on Pain, People and Power.* At the same time, I was hustling my photography skills taking pictures at parties, baby showers, conferences, and weddings. With my experience as an IT professional, I began helping business owners develop their online brand by building websites. I was doing all this while still working a 9-5 job. I was earning a six-figure salary at my day job, but I was miserable.

Deep in my heart, I knew the relationship with my job was over, but I was scared to break up because I was too worried about what others would think if I told them I was leaving to create a business. I think a lot of professionals want to divorce their job but hesitate out of fear, lack of financial preparation, or poor business development. But career rehab concepts like creating a career blueprint, building your brand by dating jobs, networking like a hustler, and getting paid through money, power, and respect apply just as much when you are creating a business brand. In this chapter, I'll show you how dropping out of your career could be the best move you ever make.

The Career Dropout Transition

For the past ten years, I have aspired to be a career dropout while working a regular job. Some years I have been a corporate rebel, but within the past few years especially I have been trying extremely hard to be a career dropout. There's nothing more discouraging than going to a job you hate every day knowing you have a dream or a business that you can't give your full attention to. But I think it's so important to try to transition gradually into full-time entrepreneurship and start building the dream while you are still working. The road is not easy, but while you Rehab YOU on your career rehab journey, you can Rehab YOUR BUSINESS as you develop your business idea. Most business ideas will be for either a product or service, although sometimes you may offer both within your business model.

When you Rehab YOUR BUSINESS, you will develop a solid product or service by going through the following four stages, just as you did for your career rehab process:

1. *Design (Ideation).* Create or define your business idea; identify whether you plan to sell products or services.

2. *Build (Branding)*. Brand your business with a logo, business name, slogan, or tag line. Create descriptions for your business's products or services.

3. *Test (Marketing)*. Identify your customers or clients and use online marketing tools, like a website, social media networks, paid advertisements, and email subscription technologies, to reach current and potential customers.

4. *Launch (Selling)*. As you launch your business, provide packages, online specials, and incentives to new or returning customers.

Your design (ideation) phase is always happening in the background, since you are likely thinking about ways to start your new venture as you prepare to transition out of your job and into your new solo gig. But the other three stages might need a bit more explanation. Let's cover some of the issues you may face as you brand, test, and launch your new venture.

Brand Your Business Idea

For most new entrepreneurs, branding is the hardest part of starting a business. You may have an idea of what you want your logo to look like and what your business name should be. But making that vision come to light can be a long and difficult process. Early in my journey, I had a hard time finding a good but cost-effective logo designer and website designer. Although as an IT professional I had the knowledge and experience to do the technical work, I did not have the time. Since you will be the face of your business in the beginning, it's important to learn how to outsource the brand development to others who can make your idea come to life.

Remember that you will need to register your business and protect it with a trademark or patent. About five years ago I stumbled across the online tools and legal services listed below, which have really helped me brand and legally protect my career coaching business and digital technology business. I have personally used the following for logo design, website design, fliers, business registration, and business tax ID registration:

- → *Fiverr.* The cheapest online freelancer platform that connects you with logo designers, website designers, writers, book cover designers, mobile app developers, etc.
- → *99designs.* Another online freelance platform that connects clients to designers, where you submit design requirements for your project and multiple graphic designers compete for your business.
- → *LegalZoom.* An awesome legal technology company that will help you register your business, business tax ID, patents, trademarks, copyrights, etc.
- → *Trademarkia.* Another online legal resource, where you can find attorneys to help you register your trademarks and patents.

Market Your Product or Service

Once you get your business logo and website created, you will be ready to start marketing your products or services. But before you just jump out there and start selling your business, you should sit down and plan a marketing strategy, the same way you developed a job search strategy for yourself. You first need to identify where your potential customers are, either online or in person. One of the most common ways for business owners to fail is to just start marketing to everyone without being strategic about who they target.

In the beginning, hiring a marketing firm to help may not be in your budget. Fortunately, there are many free marketing tools you can use to help execute your business marketing strategy. Below, I have listed ten free marketing tools I have used to market my personal and business brands over the past decade:

1. *Hootsuite.* Offers a limited free plan that allows you to manage up to three social media profiles. You can schedule up to 30 social media posts to market your products and services.
2. *Social media business pages.* You can create a free business social media profile on LinkedIn, Facebook, Twitter, YouTube, and Instagram to promote your business.

3. *Mailchimp.* Free email marketing tool for your website that collects email addresses for an online database, which you can use to market newsletters and ads to your customers.

4. *Google Analytics.* Google's web analytics tool can track your website visitors from every state, country, mobile device, and internet browser. It's a great way to assess where your customers are located, anywhere in the world.

5. *WordPress.* A content management system that offers free themes to help you create a website or blog for your business.

6. *Yoast SEO Plugin.* An addition to WordPress websites and blogs that will improve organic search rankings on Google, Yahoo! and Bing.

7. *Canva.* Free graphics editing software you can use to create images for your social media posts, blog content, and website pages.

8. *Bing Places for Business.* A free service through the Bing search engine that allows you to list your business online.

9. *Google Search Console.* A resource that allows you to submit your website to the Google search engine. The service improves your SEO and identifies errors that could potentially hurt your Google rankings.

10. *Craigslist.* A free site that allows you to list your products for sale and market your business services in your city/state, depending on your location.

Your personal brand or business is valuable, so make sure you take advantage of these free or low-cost tools and make money doing what you love. With a strong commitment and a starter budget, you can market your business brand, products, and services to millions using your computer and mobile device. All you have to do is create the brand and post it online. You are just one click away—go for it.

Sell Your Product or Service

As you prepare to divorce your job and marry your dream, it's vital that you start setting sales performance metrics and goals for your products and services. While you are still working, try to project your monthly income based on sales. Don't divorce your job so early that you become unable to pay your bills. Your career divorce may require financial sacrifices: You may not be able to go shopping as frequently, or you may have to pay off your credit-card debt or your car loan before you leave your job. Entrepreneurship means both freedom and sacrifice. Until your business revenues match your annual salary, you may have to work a little longer—but being able to create products and services that sell is the key to divorcing your job faster.

As an author, speaker, and technologist, I have thoroughly examined new ways to make money while working in the IT industry. As much as I want to be a full-time entrepreneur, I know I need to learn the art of selling my books, products, and self like the larger, well-known brands. You must stay connected and develop a selling strategy that fits your products and services. Try these ten ways to sell your product or service:

1. Create an online store on your business website.
2. Sell your products using Shopify, a popular ecommerce platform.
3. Create a merchant account on Amazon to market your products.
4. Sell your products using a mobile application that is built specifically for your company.
5. Create a referral-based system to sell your services to new and existing customers.
6. Conduct live webinars and video seminars and sell your services on YouTube, Facebook Live, and Instagram's IGTV.
7. Create alliances with other popular business owners and online influencers and get them to share your products and services.
8. Sell your expertise by marketing your products and services at speaking engagements.
9. Sell your expertise by appearing on popular podcast shows.

10. Become a vendor at conferences and events so you can sell your products and services to attendees.

Build Your Business While You Work

When you are in a bad career situation or feel that you are ready to divorce your job to marry your dream, consider what new skills you can acquire while working that would benefit your business. What training could you get your company to pay for that would benefit your brand and marketing strategy? You have to constantly wear your hustler hat and think strategically, because your job and business can benefit from your professional development enhancements. Try these tips to grow your business while still working a day job:

→ Work for a company that sells products or services similar to your business idea.

→ Ask your job to send you to training that will help you learn how to better brand, market, and sell your products and services.

→ Build your business's online following by leveraging your existing professional network on Facebook, LinkedIn, Twitter, Instagram, etc.

→ Read related books, blogs, and articles daily that will help your business grow.

→ Listen to business podcast shows where other entrepreneurs share their stories of setbacks, failures, and successes.

→ Attend local business meetups and conferences where you can learn the ins and outs of selling your products and services in your area.

→ Learn how to find funding for your business through loans, angel investors, and grants.

→ Begin to build your team by identifying professionals in your network who could help your business grow.

As you practice these moves to grow and scale, remember that your ultimate goal is to convert your brand into a business. My friend Stephen Hart shares some insights below for how to do that.

Turn Your Personal Brand into a Business
with insights from Stephen A. Hart, Founder of Isles Media LLC, Host of the Trailblazers.FM Podcast, and brand alignment strategist

Once you have developed clarity around your personal brand, it's natural to begin to monetize your offerings and turn your brand into a business. In fact, you're often able to create multiple streams of income using your personal brand and offerings. Some of your offerings might include:

→ Public speaking
→ Sponsorships
→ Consulting
→ Coaching
→ Live events
→ Online/live courses
→ Physical products
→ Books

Weekly Posting for Your Personal Brand

Stephen also recommends marketing your personal and business brands on LinkedIn. LinkedIn only averages 3 million posts weekly, but it has more than 9 billion *impressions* each week. This is a huge opportunity for you to share your wisdom with others and get in front of your target audience.

Post in different formats on a regular basis (at least two times per week):

→ Quote-based posts
→ How-to/list-based articles
→ Short videos
→ Images/infographics

Hustlers Build Businesses
with insights from Kenneth L. Johnson,
President of East Coast Executives

Building a successful business is way harder than building a successful career. I often chat with fellow career coaches who know the struggle of creating a business that helps professionals just like you. I sat down and chatted with my good friend Kenneth L. Johnson, who is a career hustler in its purest essence.

Kenneth began his career journey in Philadelphia, where he had a dream of owning a staffing firm. There was a 15-block radius in Philly where all the big players in the staffing industry operated. So with no experience, his approach needed to be both enterprising and strategic. Kenneth found out the key to being an effective "business hustler" was to do impeccable research and offer a unique value to your clientele. In this case, his clientele were the office managers, regional managers, and owners of area staffing/recruitment firms. Kenneth is a diversity recruitment professional who provides training, career development resources, and job placement for minority professionals.

With a defined strategy, resume, and elevator pitch in hand, he set out to make his mark in the Philadelphia staffing and recruitment world. It paid off: He is the president of East Coast Executives, the world's leading diversity recruitment firm, now based in Harlem, New York. The journey to this point hasn't been easy, but Kenneth believes the key to success is to establish a secure enough network to avoid consistent losses and always possess enough social capital (i.e., clients) to avoid a prolonged drought.

The most common and valuable characteristic of a successful hustler is their ability to network. Just the thought of networking scares most people, and many who claim to be expert networkers often just talk too much. Kenneth told me, "You don't have to be a go-getter or even aggressive, but you better be an active listener if you want to grow your brand." To be successful in business, you have to sell, market, and pitch well enough to survive. The most admired executives and professionals have mastered the ability to market their individual brand and align it with the needs of their prospects and customers to the point that they are seen as invaluable. Now those are hustlers!

Kenneth said, "Relationships are human currency. Your network is your net worth—it's not who you know but who knows you." All this is true *and* false because relationships are based on people, and people change, in life and in business. This is important, because it mitigates disappointment and the up-and-down cycles that are synonymous with business relationships. Here are the six relationships Kenneth believes you need to succeed in business:

1. *Connection.* The person who presents the opportunity.
2. *Customer.* They are the lifeline of any successful business venture.
3. *Mentor.* An experienced or trusted advisor—someone who has knowledge of the journey and is willing to share and offer advice openly.
4. *Sponsor.* Whether they're external or internal, a sponsor will speak positively about you and stand up for you when you're not in the room.
5. *Truth Teller.* Success is intoxicating, but what you perceive isn't always a true reflection of reality. This is the person who checks you.
6. *Cheerleader.* It takes two to celebrate. The cheerleader provides a positive spin on your successes, concerns, and challenges. They're the one you call when you need someone to listen.

Networking When You Drop Out and Go Solo

The way we network is changing, and how you network when you are building a career may be different from how you network when building a new business. As the focus becomes more on social media and other online networking, the tried-and-true method of face-to-face networking appears to be diminishing in value. I believe you can build a virtual network, but you must still construct the foundation on personal interactions. We're operating in a global economy and we may not be able to meet everyone we work with, but even a brief phone call can solidify a relationship, close a deal, or simply spark the beginning of a friendship. This is the key piece for hustlers who are starting a business: It's a calculated game of rapid-fire decisions, and those decisions will seem much clearer when you're looking your customer, colleague, or business partner in the face and shaking their hand to close the deal.

As a business owner, it can sometimes be difficult to connect with potential customers and clients or to create partnerships with other business owners. But social media is one of the most powerful ways to begin to build connections with other hustlers and learn from successful brands. Once you have made these online contacts, you can connect with them face to face, via phone, or through email. Here are four ways to network online as a business owner:

1. Join Facebook and LinkedIn groups for business owners.
2. Join Facebook and LinkedIn groups where your potential clients or customers may need your services or products.
3. Connect with like-minded business owners, CEOs, or CFOs online and then add them as friends or professional contacts on LinkedIn, Facebook, Twitter, and Instagram.
4. Conduct weekly conference calls, coffee chats, or virtual meetings with other business owners and potential customers.

Exit Strategy: Divorce the Job

When you are truly ready to divorce your 9-5 job, you may experience many emotions, including fear, anxiety, or stress, as you execute your exit strategy. Here's how you can prepare:

- *Mentally.* Try to remain calm and patient as you close out this chapter in your life. Don't allow your mind to play tricks on you; be courageous and brave.
- *Financially.* Saving money before you try running your business full time will ease some of the anxiety and stress. Try to have 6 to 12 months of savings so you can easily pay your bills.
- *Physically.* Sign up for cost-effective health-care insurance for business owners. If your spouse works, you can take advantage of their benefits instead.
- *Spiritually.* You will need to keep the faith during discouraging times, so stay rounded in your spirituality. Pray or meditate often to keep your mind, spirit, and emotions full of positive energy. The road to a successful business requires you to be resilient, and you will need to persevere through any and all setbacks and failures.

Career divorce is never easy, but career rehab is all about restoring and rebuilding what you need for a sustainable future. With proper preparation, you can build a solid company, but the journey may not be easy. Remember you have a personal brand to fall back on if you ever decide to go back to a 9-5 job. That's the beauty in stepping out on faith: There isn't much to fear, knowing you can rely on your education, experience, and expertise, whether as an employee or an entrepreneur. Business skills like product development, sales, marketing, and consulting are transferable if you have to go back to the 9-5 life. Career dropouts can always go back to being corporate rebels because your personal brand will never die if you network like a hustler and market yourself and your business like an AD.

The power to succeed is already inside you—all you have to do is believe in the power of career rehab. It's a lifetime journey for your career and your business. Keep evolving, and never stop being a student of your business.

☆ Meet Mario Armstrong, Emmy Award–Winner and Entrepreneur, Host of the *Wake Up and Level Up* Podcast and Executive Producer and Host of the *Never Settle Show*

Mario Armstrong, entrepreneur and broadcaster, is a contributor to NBC and appears regularly on the *The Today Show* talking about tech, entrepreneurship, and personal brand coaching.

☆ *When did you know you were ready to divorce the 9-5 life for your dream?*

☆ I knew I was ready to leave the 9-5 when I was able to understand how the dream could be monetized. I left my corporate career 12 years ago to pursue this passion, and I asked my wife to leave her job and run our company as CEO, which she did. We went broke together pursuing our dream when the recession hit, and we had to fight and scrape to get by. Our 401(k) was gone, credit cards were maxed, and we were also trying to raise our 5-year-old son at the time. We stayed resilient—when one of us was down, the other one had to be up. It was during this time that we came up with the idea of the *Never Settle Show* to empower others with real stories of inspiration and the blueprint on how they overcame obstacles. Our resilience was rewarded by winning an Emmy for the *Never Settle Show* in its first season.

After realizing that the side hustle was working, I was acquiring sponsors and obtaining distribution, which showed me the real potential. I was making decent progress without leaving the job. When my wife, Nicole, came onboard, she created pricing models that really maximized the value I was putting out there but not monetizing to its fullest. Once I got that first $10,000 speaking engagement, I was like, "Oh, this is REAL."

☆ *What preparation should be in place before a professional becomes a career dropout (leaves their job) to pursue entrepreneurship?*

☆ I advise five steps before leaving your job to pursue entrepreneurship:

1. *Build the side hustle while you have the day job* (unless your day job is bad for your health); you don't want to just jump off the cliff and try to build wings on the way

Mario Armstrong, continued

down. It's stressful and creates a ton of friction, and that creates an environment for bad decisions. You need to side hustle on weekends, after work hours, and taking days off from work—whatever it takes.

2. *Get real customers.* You need to genuinely identify that you have something that actually solves a problem, and not just because your family and friends say so. In other words, you need real customers. Prove that you can get actual customers first.

3. *Intentionality.* You must be intentional about choosing a date for this transition to happen. The date needs to give you some time to plan your exit and map out necessary goals. Set the date and then work backwards with the goals you need to accomplish.

4. *Proper savings.* Don't take the advice of a year's worth of savings; it's not enough of a runway. Entrepreneurship is about staying flexible, building resilience, and when you first start out, it's all about staying alive.

5. *And don't overlook the possibility of your current employer becoming a customer.* This won't fit for everyone, but for many of you it could be a missed opportunity, especially if you were a valuable employee.

Q *What if a business owner designs, builds, tests, and launches a product or service and it still fails? What advice would you give them to help them never give up? How can we condition our mindsets to never settle?*

A The average person usually settles or gives up. Too many give up too soon. They are so close, but if you don't have the systems and clarity in place, the big picture becomes quickly overwhelming. In my opinion, you only fail when you don't try or didn't learn from it. Learning from our attempts helps inform us for the next move. We won an Emmy for the *Never Settle Show* because every time we were knocked down we'd get back up. To develop a never-settle mindset, you have to want to train your brain, develop a harmonious environment, and have strong determination. Our brains by default are wired to protect us from risk, to look out for things that seem scary. Going on your own can be scary, and that enables the inner critic to start telling you why you can't accomplish your dream. It's not about who you are—it's what you tell yourself you aren't. So starting with positive self-talk is critical. In neuroscience

Mario Armstrong, continued

there is something called the reticular activating system (RAS), a collection of nerves in your brainstem that filters out unnecessary information so the essential stuff makes it through. Your RAS takes whatever you focus heavily on and develops a filter for it. If you train your RAS to look for good, you will find more good. If you constantly complain, your RAS will look for more things for you to complain about. The RAS is why you start seeing that red car you want everywhere. It's also the reason that you can be in a crowded event with a lot of noise but shift to immediate attention if you think you hear your name being called from across the room. Knowing our brain does this means you can hack it by feeding it positive reinforcement and reminding yourself of your potential every day. Creating a supportive and harmonious environment enables your brain training to be extremely successful.

It's very hard to tell yourself positive reinforcement when other aspects of your life are in chaos. It's important to get as much of your life in order before venturing out on your own, and if you have family members who are dream killers, you need to let them know how they are affecting you and ask for their love and support, but not their validation. Your family are shareholders of your company. So one tip is to get the family involved in doing a vision board of your goals with you. Having your shareholders contribute to the vision board is a powerful tool to get them to understand the goal and the sacrifices it will take to get there. As part of creating a successful environment, it's time for you to do the tough thing and cut relationships with negative people. Negative people have a problem for every solution! Lastly, you need the one superpower that keeps you going: determination. Doing things that need to be done even when you don't feel like it is the definition of determination. Your actions must match your ambition. There will be plenty of days where you feel like throwing in the towel or when you can't seem to muster up the energy—these are exactly the moments where your inner strength, faith, and determination must kick in. Determination is the one superpower that can truly demonstrate progress.

⭐ *Were there any career roles, heartbreaks, or situations that helped you get the mindset for entrepreneurship?*

⭐ Yes, the best career role to get you ready for entrepreneurship is sales. Get some sales training. The other key situation and strategy is to work in the industry you intend to

Mario Armstrong, continued

be an entrepreneur in. That will give you a massive advantage before going on your own. If you can't switch industries to your passion, then look for roles or projects that you can volunteer on at your current employer that have the skill sets you'll need when you go on your own. Ask if you can shadow a co-worker in a different department for the day; ask if you can work on a project that wouldn't typically involve you. These tactics will help get you the exposure, training, and skills you've identified as important for you to acquire for your entrepreneurial success.

16

☆ ☆ ☆

STAY FOCUSED
ON YOU

Your career rehab journey does not end when you finish reading this book. It will begin over and over as you renovate new areas of your career. When you start a new job, that's a new journey; when you make a career change, that's a new journey, too. All new beginnings are a new journey in our lives. We can't go back to settling for less and dealing with toxic cultures, bad managers, and unworkable deadlines. You have the power to determine your own destiny. But it's up to you to be realistic about what you want for your life, career, and business. Everyone should have a life outside their career, and if they want to start a business, they can have that, too. Nothing is impossible when you stay focused on creating career happiness for yourself. Your career happiness is your responsibility, and you have to cherish it the same way you love your family and children. There is no career decision too hard for you to make when you create, market, and sell your personal brand. In this chapter, we'll talk about how you can keep the focus on YOU.

Focus on Continuous Career Restoration

Our careers need constant improvement and continuous restoration each year. Career rehab is a lifetime journey as a professional and business owner. You must constantly gut out the bad stuff and replace it with new skills and new experience. As you grow as a professional, you will be able to easily identify what to eliminate and whether it's time to date a new job. In your job interviews and networking, you will recognize the good company cultures and professionals who can help your career evolve. After dumping bad jobs a few times, you will come to recognize what you want in a career relationship and realize when you want to marry your dream and divorce your career. But you have to be willing to make those decisions even when it feels scary. Being honest with yourself will give you the strength to know it's OK when career experiences go bad, but it's not OK to stay.

In the IT industry, we conduct continuous software deployments. This means we constantly push new code for the functionality of an application. It's the same with your career: You have to continue to make changes to help your personal brand stand out. Agile software deployments produce small amounts of new code without compromising quality. For you, this means you should constantly take professional training and continuously deploy what you learn to help your career without sacrificing your commute time and personal happiness.

Don't Neglect YOU

As a professional, you may have a tendency to neglect who you are and what you want. When you quit on yourself, you are compromising what you want for your career by putting the job first when it may not always put you first. Remember to do a hard eight hours and go home on time every day. Also remember to never neglect your physical and mental health to satisfy the job. This can lead to stress, anxiety, and depression. When you neglect yourself, you will be no good to your job or your family. Career rehab requires self care and family care. Beyond your job, the only thing that really matters in this life is you and your family. A job can always replace you, but you can't replace yourself and your loved ones. I like to think of career rehab as a daily progression toward being able to control your life and your career, without having to choose just one.

Unlearn Bad Career Habits

You can stay focused on rehabbing you when you understand how to unlearn bad career habits. The process of unlearning these habits requires you to gut out the bad stuff you don't like about yourself before you can restore your career. And restoration can't take place without reflecting on what went well and what went badly with past career moves.

☆ Meet Barry O'Reilly,
Entrepreneur and Author of *Unlearn:*
Let Go of Past Success to Achieve Extraordinary Results

Barry O'Reilly is a business advisor, entrepreneur, and author who has pioneered the intersection of business model innovation, product development, organizational design, and culture transformation with both disruptive startups and Fortune 500 behemoths. He is author of two books, *Unlearn: Let Go of Past Success to Achieve Extraordinary Results*, and *Lean Enterprise: How High Performance Organizations Innovate at Scale*. He is an internationally

Barry O'Reilly, continued

sought-after speaker, frequent writer, and contributor to *The Economist, Strategy+Business,* and *MIT Sloan Management Review.*

Barry is faculty at Singularity University, advising and contributing to Singularity's executive and accelerator programs based in San Francisco and throughout the globe. He is also founder of ExecCamp, the entrepreneurial experience for executives, and management consultancy Antennae.

Q: How can professionals unlearn bad career habits through commitment and courage?

A: Courage is the recognition that what you are doing is not working for you, letting go, and taking action to do what is needed to progress.

The first breakthrough is the realization that you must, in fact, unlearn. By identifying the aspiration or outcome you wish to achieve—paired with the deliberate practice to get there—you can start to move toward your desired state and achieve extraordinary results.

Adopting the cycle of unlearning doesn't rely on being smart, or lucky, or desperate, or all of the above. It relies only on you—your courage and commitment to use it intentionally in your work and your life to achieve extraordinary results. Do you have the courage to recognize that what you are doing is not working, be willing to accept it, let go, and try something different? What aspirations do you have but feel unclear about where to start? Have you set expectations of yourself but not delivered your desired outcome, citing excuses or hardships you know you're unwilling to face? What challenge are you struggling with, and you've tried all your tools yet still seem stuck? These are clear signals you are limiting your performance or have hit a local maximum, and that it's time to begin the cycle of unlearning.

Q: How can professionals relearn new methods, behaviors, and thinking that will help them create a successful career?

A: By exploring difficult tasks, you will discover a tremendous amount about yourself. You'll understand your mind and body's natural resistance, as well as the discipline and power of deliberate practice to overcome internal and external obstacles to succeed. You'll build your own personal resilience and self-belief.

Barry O'Reilly, continued

But there are immense challenges to relearning effectively, and we create many of these challenges ourselves. First, you must be willing to adapt and be open to

information that goes against your inherent beliefs—that may be at odds with what you have always been told or taught to do. Second, you may need to learn how to learn again. Finally, you must create an environment for relearning to happen in a meaningful, yet often challenging, space outside your existing comfort zone.

As you unlearn your current limiting but ingrained methods, behaviors, and thinking, you can take in new data, information, and perspectives. And by considering all this new input, you naturally challenge your existing mental models of the world. It is by leveraging these insights that you can seek improvement, adaptation, and growth.

⭐ *What is the best way for professionals to understand career breakthroughs? How can they let go of existing mental models, methods, and past career achievements?*

⭐ Highly effective leaders are constantly searching for inspiration and new ideas. But before any real breakthroughs can happen, we need to step away from the old models, mindsets, and behaviors that are limiting our potential and current performance. We must unlearn what brought us success in the past to find continued success in the future.

The first breakthrough is the realization that you must, in fact, unlearn. Leaders believe they simply need to tell people to think differently, and they will act differently. This is a fallacy that must, in fact, be unlearned. The way to think differently is to act differently. When you act differently, you start to see and experience the world differently, impacting your mindset as a result. And because you're realizing the benefits of adapting your behaviors and gaining new perspectives that impact your mindset, you become open to unlearning your behaviors more often. It's an accelerant.

As we break free of our existing mental models and methods, we learn to let go of the past to achieve extraordinary results. We realize that as the world is constantly evolving, innovating, and progressing, so too must we. Persisting with the same thinking and behaviors inhibits ongoing and future success.

Barry O'Reilly, continued

Our breakthroughs provide an opportunity to reflect on the lessons we have learned from relearning and provide a springboard for tackling bigger and more audacious challenges. This process can be as simple as asking yourself what went well, not so well, and what you would do differently if you were to try and unlearn the same challenge again. Using this information and insight and feeding it forward to future loops of the cycle of unlearning means every loop of the cycle results in deeper insight, greater impact, and growth.

Q: *How can professionals stay focused on their career rehab journey and not stop relearning the definition of success?*

A: By continuously defining and redefining success in terms of the outcomes or aspirations they want to achieve. If you don't define success before you start to experiment with new skills, roles, and responsibilities, it's going to be very difficult to hold yourself accountable to understand if you're moving in your desired direction.

Defining success before you start helps to set your definition of where you want to be. It enables you to set expectations with yourself, your peers, and your collaborators of where you want to be. Without defining your outcomes before you start, you'll have no navigation tool for the uncertainty you're about to face. So do it, review and adapt it as you learn what you like and don't like, and learn, unlearn, and relearn along the way.

Don't Give Up on Your Dreams

One of the biggest misperceptions about being a full-time professional is that most of us have felt or still feel pressured to give up on our personal dreams. You can have a successful career *and* you can chase your dreams. One of my managers would always tell me, "Kanika, you can have it all." I would look at him like he was crazy. But he was right. Writing a book and getting a publishing deal has been a dream of mine for more than four years, and as you read this chapter, you can see it has come true. I still have dreams of speaking in front of huge audiences and helping them build their personal brand and change how they work. These dreams are actually coming true. In August 2019 I spoke at Microsoft at a Women in Tech event. The AnitaB.org event was amazing. The speaking topic was "How to Level Up in Tech." I encouraged so many women to rehab their personal brands for their dream jobs within the tech industry.

But you can only have it all if you are willing to fight for it. We give so much to our careers and don't give the same time or effort to our dreams. The sacrifice is worth it to develop your dream product or service. Fulfilling that passion may require you to give up on that toxic job for a job that will bring you more happiness and bring you closer to your dream.

When you give up on your dream, you are not staying focused on career happiness. Remember, this journey is not a destination. It may not happen overnight, but don't give up. You can do it if you believe and work hard enough, and it should be easier because you are motivated by your passions and purpose. The art of never quitting requires you to fight every setback as you follow your dreams. Professionals are educated people with dreams of being great. And now you can unlock the door to your greatness, use the "good bones" of your brand, and rehab and renovate your career into what you've only dreamed it could be.

☆ ☆ ☆

ABOUT THE AUTHOR

Kanika Tolver is the CEO and founder of Career Rehab, LLC in Washington, DC. Career Rehab focuses on assisting career transformations for students, professionals, and retirees. Her company provides career coaching programs, events, webinars, and digital resources to help people reach their career goals.

Tolver is an in-demand coach, consultant, speaker, and thought leader who is often tapped as an expert source for the media, having been featured on CNN, CBS Radio, Yahoo!, and Glassdoor and in Entrepreneur, *The Washington Post*, and a variety of radio interviews. She specializes in helping individuals establish themselves as the "architects of their own lives" and realize career, business, life, and spiritual success—all in a way that promotes restoration, balance, and nurturing of one's authentic self. A self-professed "tech geek" and career technologist enamored by the latest and greatest gadgetry, Tolver is also an advocate of "people of color" becoming more involved in science and technology.

Tolver is also the author of the acclaimed title *Life Rehab: Don't Overdose on Pain, People and Power*. She graduated from Bowie State University in Maryland and currently hails from Washington, DC, where she has lived for most of her life. She enjoys spending time with her husband, family, and friends.

☆ ☆ ☆

INDEX